Unrevealed Until Its Season

a lenten journey with hymns

James C. Howell

UPPER ROOM BOOKS®
NASHVILLE

Contents

First Week in Lent
Merciful and Mighty: HYMNS PRAISING GOD

Second Week in Lent
Beautiful Savior: HYMNS ABOUT JESUS

Third Week in Lent
Prone to Wander: HYMNS OF FORGIVENESS

Fourth Week in Lent
Thy Presence My Light: HYMNS OF VISION

Fifth Week in Lent
With Joy Surround You: HYMNS OF BEAUTY

Sixth Week in Lent
Stony the Road: HYMNS OF HOLY WEEK

Easter
Love's Redeeming Work: HYMNS OF EASTER

In the Bulb There Is a Flower

$\mathcal{A}$ chance remark at a church covered-dish dinner awakened something surprising in me. A guy I barely knew asked me what my favorite phrase in a hymn might be. Not my favorite hymn, but a phrase *in* a hymn. As I stumbled, he shared his: "The hopes and fears of all the years are met in thee tonight." I couldn't get that phrase out of my head for days. So much is there, such psychological and theological depth. And in a single phrase.

Hymns had always spoken deeply to me. I began to unravel why. The best hymns are profound poetry that hints at more than it states on the surface—and I began to see how hymns sung over a lifetime instill godly wisdom and dramatic insights for living without us even noticing. Hymns embed faith into the soul more vividly than words merely spoken or read.

"The hopes and fears of all the years" prompted me to write a book about Christmas carols. It was not about who wrote them or why but instead the astonishing surplus of meaning hiding in phrases we've sung forever: "Sing all ye citizens of heaven above," "Mary, Joseph, lend your aid," and "Why lies he in such mean estate." I pledged to myself to do the same for hymns from the rest of the year, especially Lent. This book is the result.

The way pregnant phrases in hymns work is illustrated in a relatively new one, "The Hymn of Promise." The first line ushers us outside to ponder three marvels in nature. "In the bulb there is a flower; in the seed, an apple tree; in cocoons . . . butterflies." The beauty to come is hidden for a long time in something that looks nothing like what will be. Bulbs and cocoons are brownish and dirty; who would ever imagine that flowers and butterflies are gestating in there? A seed is tiny; who would dream it could become something tall and sturdy like a tree?

The genius of so many hymns is that a poet, who we might even dare to suggest was inspired by God, evokes an image. It's not overexplained. It rustles around in the soul and takes on an unexpected life, unique to each singer and yet shared by all. This was the genius of Jesus the storyteller. He never carved in stone seven things you'd better believe. Instead he pointed to a sower, a pearl merchant, a shrub, and a father's embrace, teasing his listeners to poke around and find something beautiful.

Hymns have a big advantage over Jesus' words: the music. Anywhere, anytime, if you hear the first three notes of "Amazing Grace" or "Hymn of Promise," your soul awakens and rises up to a memory, a moment, a dream, so much love, and an inexplicable sense of God's presence and peace. Something unrevealed is revealed first in the tune and then in the words. Each of these reflections lingers over some phrase you've sung but have likely never explored. Some of these phrases even hold the underlying plot of the entire hymn. There's a flower in that bulb. There's "a song in every silence, seeking word and melody." Like the two disciples on the road to Emmaus, our eyes are opened, our hearts are inflamed, we recognize the risen Lord, and we begin to understand the scriptures (see Luke 24:28-32). In death we see resurrection and hope. We catch a glimpse of "something God alone can see."

Suggestions for How to Use This Book

Think of this Lenten study like a Bible study with hymns instead of scripture. You are probably familiar with most of these hymns, just like you are probably familiar with most Bible stories, but you will get more out of the devotional if you go to the source before and after reading the day's meditation. With hymns you can read lyrics, play music, sing, or listen to recordings. These hymns are all readily available in hymnals such as *The United Methodist Hymnal* (UMH) and on streaming services like YouTube. Try different combinations of reading lyrics and listening to recordings of the day's hymn before and after the meditation. You will quickly find what works for you.

Hymn Titles and, When Available, UMH Numbers

Day 1: "When I Survey the Wondrous Cross" (299)
Day 2: "Take My Life, and Let It Be" (399)
Day 3: "(We Are Climbing) Jacob's Ladder" (418)
Day 4: "He Leadeth Me: O Blessed Thought" (128)
First Sunday in Lent: "Holy, Holy, Holy" (64)
Day 5: "Here I Am, Lord" (593)
Day 6: "O God, Our Help in Ages Past" (117)
Days 7 and 8: "How Great Thou Art" (77)
Day 9: "A Mighty Fortress Is Our God" (110)
Day 10: "Near to the Heart of God" (472)
Second Sunday in Lent: "Fairest Lord Jesus" (189)
Day 11: "Lord, You Have Come to the Lakeshore" (344)
Day 12: "Break Thou the Bread of Life" (599)
Day 13: "What a Friend We Have in Jesus" (526)
Day 14: "Jesus, Lover of My Soul" (479)
Day 15: "Rock of Ages, Cleft for Me" (361)
Day 16: "Jesus Loves Me" (191)

ASH WEDNESDAY

When I Survey

When our Ash Wednesday service has ended, I linger in front of a mirror, not to inspect the quality of the pastor's smudge above my eyes, but to ponder that I have just been marked with the horror and hope of Jesus' cross. No other hymn captures so thrillingly the paradox of this horror and hope as Isaac Watts's "When I Survey the Wondrous Cross." We "survey" the cross. We don't just glance at it. We measure it carefully, size it up, consider every angle.

Too often, we sanitize the cross, preferring those of smooth wood or shiny metal. The original cross would have been of olive wood, gnarled with human flesh nailed to it. Crucifixion was a gruesome, horrifyingly painful, public humiliation of criminals. Having seen plenty of crosses, the soldiers at the foot of Jesus' cross didn't "survey" this one. They didn't know there was any reason to be attentive to this one. They could not see that this was God and that this was the start of a revolution of redemption. Jesus looked like any other dying, despised person—which was precisely what God wanted to achieve.

"See, from his head, his hands, his feet, sorrow and love flow mingled down." Just meditate on that for a minute, or an hour, or the rest of your life. Blood and perspiration were mingled all over his ravaged body. After the piercing by the soldier's cruel lance, blood and water flowed, mingled down.

Back then, observers might have assumed it was some mingling of justice and tragedy. But no, it was sorrow and love mingled; God's eternal, fully manifested love for us mingled with sorrow over our brokenness, our waywardness, our confusion, and our mortality. Medieval paintings depict little angels flying around the cross with cups to catch that sorrow and love flowing down. It's precious. It's medicine. It's life for the world.

"Did e'er . . . thorns compose so rich a crown?" At the coronation of Elizabeth II, the Archbishop of Canterbury placed St. Edward's Crown on her head. It was heavy, forged of 22-karat gold, with 444 precious stones, including aquamarines, topazes, rubies, amethysts, and sapphires. She then knelt to receive the body and blood of our Lord. Did she ponder Jesus' very different crown, its only ornaments those harsh thorns gashing his forehead, scalp, and temples?

This cross isn't just some religious artifact. It is much more than the mechanism God uses to get you into heaven once you've died. It fundamentally alters our values and how we live. If this is God, if the heart of God was fully manifest in this moment, if this is what God's love actually looks like, then everything changes. "My richest gain I count but loss" (echoing Paul's words in Philippians 3:8). "Pour contempt on all my pride." "Forbid it Lord that I should boast, save in the death of Christ" (echoing Paul's other words in Galatians 6:14). "All the vain things that charm me most, I sacrifice them."

Indeed, the more we ponder the crucified Lord on the cross, the less attached we are to the gadgets and baubles of this world. We give up things for Lent as a training exercise to make us ready to abandon whatever we cling to. It is as if someone at the foot of the cross were reading the book of Ecclesiastes aloud: "Vanity of vanities! All is vanity" (1:2). Indeed.

Casting aside vain fantasies, we don't sing this hymn and then hurry back into our old life. We get caught up in Christ's causes and become generous with our money and things. What is your offering to God? "Were the whole realm of nature mine" (an absurd idea, that the richest of the rich could have so much!), "that were an offering far too small." No gift we could muster would be enough to begin to match Christ's sacrificial gift to us.

So why then is my giving so measured, so chintzy? Why do I think of the life of faith as only somewhat important? Why is God the one I neglect until I'm in a pickle? The last words of the hymn get to the truth of things and stand as a stirring, unavoidable challenge to us, if we sing with any sincerity at all: "Love so amazing, so divine, demands my soul, my life, my all." Not this compartment of my soul, or this segment of my life, or the part of me I don't mind parting with. My soul. My life. My all.

Take My Moments

$\mathcal{A}$s a young pastor, I would jokingly needle people about their lack of candor as they would stand and sing the second stanza of "Take My Life, and Let It Be." The lyrics say clearly and as a prayer to God, "Take my silver and my gold; not a mite would I withhold." But they were withholding quite a few mites! This supposedly clever critique of mine derailed me from attending to the rest of the hymn.

For instance, "Take my moments." What's a moment? _Wait a moment. He's having a moment._ It's almost nothing, a little freeze-frame of time, ephemeral, passing as quickly as it's noticed or ignored. And yet what is life except a moment, another moment, a bunch of moments one after the other? What do I get done in just a moment anyhow? A thought, sizing up somebody, a little barb of critique in my head. Or maybe a flash of self-doubt. Or staring, gawking at . . . Well, what do I fixate on in my random moments?

In a moment, I blurt out something I should have kept to myself. Or I seize the moment and encourage somebody. In a moment I notice unexpected beauty. In a moment the doctor's verdict rocks my world. In a moment I decide something huge. Is my mind, much less my heart, able to parse moment after moment and ask God to take, fill, and use them? It would require some practice, perhaps the fixed intentionality of Lent or the kind of soul transplant that happens over a lifetime of worship, prayer, Scripture reading, and the humming of this hymn.

"Take my hands" and "take my feet." Lord, use my hands and feet! But there's more. Your hands and feet actually *are* the hands and feet of Christ. Paul, after all, said that we are the body of Christ, and that your body is the temple of the Holy Spirit (see 1 Corinthians 6:19). The hymn reminds me that my call is not merely to do something nice or for God now and then. My hands are Jesus'; my feet are Jesus'. What a privilege! What a responsibility. What pressure. What joy.

"Take my voice" and "take my lips." Your mouth is an amazing portal between out there and inside you. Your voice comes out of it. What do you say and why? Christian talk isn't sweet or sugary, but it will always say true things. Christian talk is always encouraging, never belittling. The voice does sing, even if you can't sing on pitch—and God loves our voices raised in song. The mouth eats and drinks. What do you put in there and why? The mouth expresses who you are—in a grimace, a frown, a smile, a sneer, and a kiss. Can you get in the mode of thinking that your mouth is God's and your lips are God's? Can you remember to ask if what you do with them and what passes in or out through them is it in some way "consecrated, Lord to thee"?

Back to the "silver and gold." We pretty much do what we wish with our silver and gold. Sometimes we pray for God to give us more. Sometimes we toss some spare change into the offering and feel fairly noble. What did the hymn writer have in mind? She actually told us. Frances Havergal, way back in 1873, explained that, for her personally,

> "Take my silver and my gold" now means shipping off
> all my ornaments,—including a jewel cabinet which is

really fit for a countess—to the Church Missionary Society where they will be accepted and disposed of for me. I retain only a brooch for daily wear, which is a memorial of my dear parents; also a locket with the only portrait I have of my niece in heaven, Evelyn. I had no idea I had such a jeweller's shop; nearly fifty articles are being packed off. I don't think I need tell you that I never packed a box with such pleasure.[1]

You don't have to be St. Francis and give all your worldly possessions away to sing this hymn. But what silver and gold do you have at your disposal? What would it look like to ask the church or its missionaries to dispose of it for you? Havergal withheld a mite, two mites actually, treasured family recollections. But God didn't mind. Her nice things found their true home, their godly purpose, when she released them as part of the consecration of her life. Her pleasure was in fulfilling the scripture that inspired the hymn, Romans 12:1-2: "I appeal to you therefore, brothers and sisters, by the mercies of God, to present your bodies as a living sacrifice, holy and acceptable to God, which is your spiritual worship. Do not be conformed to this world, but be transformed by the renewing of your minds, so that you may discern what is the will of God—what is good and acceptable and perfect."

Day 3

Every Rung Climbs Higher

*A*nother moment in the Bible's narrative that may expose what Lent is about, a moment when earth morphed into heaven, was Jacob's dream of a ladder (see Genesis 28), a text we cannot read with hearing a certain tune. It's hard to think of a hymn whose rhythm and melody embody what's envisioned in the hymn (and the Bible story) quite like "We Are Climbing Jacob's Ladder." Even when reading silently, we pause after "are" and after "climbing," as if grasping a rung and pulling, then pausing before the next rung. "Every rung climbs higher, higher." Singing it requires some patience. The pace is slow but certain. No wonder people enslaved on plantations, dreaming of going up and over and out of there, loved this song.

Rabbi Jonathan Sacks wrote, "Prayer is a ladder stretching from earth to heaven. On this ladder of words, thoughts and emotions, we gradually leave earth's gravitational field. We move from the world around us, perceived by the senses, to an awareness of that which lies beyond the world."[2] The days of Lent might be marked as one rung after another on this ladder.

Stephen Covey said you can spend your life climbing the ladder of success "only to discover it's leaning against the wrong wall."[3] Or there's poor Sisyphus who pushed that rock uphill, only to have it roll back down just before arriving at the summit.

Jacob had been a ladder-climber, doing whatever it took to get ahead: cheating his brother, deceiving his father, whatever. But in Genesis 28, he comes to "a certain place," no place really. He's as weary as Sisyphus and must rest. He has nothing but a rock for a pillow, although the Hebrew may imply that he put it *next to* his head for protection. There is no rest for the fearful weary. In a fitful sleep he has a dream Freud might analyze, a vision we might covet: a ladder bridging the great chasm between earth and heaven. The Hebrew really means it's a long, steep ramp, the kind archaeologists have uncovered on the sides of ziggurats in Iraq.

Angels—not the sweet, prissy kind we know from jewelry and little ceramic statues but mighty heavenly warriors and messengers—are going up and down the ramp. What could it mean? Jacob snaps out of his sleep or reverie. Dumbfounded, all he can say is "Surely the LORD is in this place—and I did not know it" (Gen. 28:16).

I wrote an entire book of recollections from my childhood, youth, and adulthood about times and places when God was present but undetected by me; only in retrospect could I see that God had been in a moment, a person, a circumstance.[4]

God was there. I not only didn't know it; I wasn't seeking it. I wasn't praying. Jacob isn't on some spiritual quest. He's not observing Lent. He's on the run from . . . his brother? His past? His demons? You don't have to be a spiritual climber to sing "We are climbing Jacob's ladder." It's as if we're groping in the dark for something but don't know what. And it turns out to be the way to God—or God's way to us. Jacob, after all, doesn't even try to climb the ladder. He's awestruck and then goes on his way to a new job, a couple of wives, children who squabble, and a lot of heartbreak. God was in those places too.

Jacob was "a border crosser, a man of liminal experiences," as Robert Alter put it.[5] We can find God—although it really is always that God is finding us—even in our restless forgetting to pray. Jacob wasn't praying, but maybe unwittingly his prayer was his brokenness, his weariness, his fitful sigh.

Standing under a fig tree, Jesus mysteriously told Nathanael, "You will see heaven opened and the angels of God ascending and descending upon the Son of Man" (John 1:51). St. Catherine of Siena thought of Jesus' crucified body as that ladder on which we climb toward God. The first rung is the nailed feet: We humbly shed our selfish will. The next rung is his open, pierced side: We press in to glimpse the abyss of divine love. Finally we scale to his face: We are moved by love to obedient holiness.

Who's doing this climbing? "Soldiers of the cross." Of course, the soldiers at Jesus' cross were the ones who nailed him to it, the ones snickering, the ones gambling over his clothing. And they were the ones he forgave, even though they didn't repent or ask for mercy. When we ponder the way God showed up to Jacob in his anxious flight from God and goodness and the way Jesus, our ladder to heaven, forgave the unrepentant soldiers of the cross, we know the only answer to the hymn's other questions: "Sinner, do you love my Jesus?" and "If you love him, why not serve him?"

His Faithful Follower
I Would Be

$\mathcal{H}$e Leadeth Me" is sung to such a cheerful tune of major chords with not a hint of dissonance that it would be easy to get lulled into feeling that God's leading is indeed a "blessed thought . . . with heavenly comfort fraught." Indeed, when God leads us, it is blessed, and there is comfort. And yet, as disciples and saints through history would be happy to remind us, being led by God can and will hurl you into conflicts, confrontations, grief, sacrifice, and even martyrdom.

And so we hesitate. We fantasize that God will lead us into green pastures, beside still waters and to a banquet of fulfillment. Joseph Henry Gilmore composed this great hymn minutes after concluding a prayer meeting focused on Psalm 23. We yearn to be cute and soft little lambs led to flowing streams by the Good Shepherd! But what is shepherding like? And what are sheep like? The first shepherd I ever saw in the Holy Land was wearing an Elvis T-shirt, slogging around in the mud in green galoshes, swatting his sheep on their hind ends with a switch, and hollering what I assumed were Arabic expletives. The Lord is my shepherd.

Sheep really are dumb. They nibble here, nibble there . . . and then they're lost. Our grave spiritual peril, one we labor to escape during Lent, is that we will dupe ourselves into believing "I'm being led by the Lord" when really, we're just enjoying life, doing nice things with nice people, basking in our health and success. With some earnestness, we do want to do God's will. But then we have a hunch, a quivering emotion inside; something appeals to us, and we think *This must be God's leading!* But is it really God, the holy and awesome God who led Abraham? Is it the God who led Moses into the forge of Pharaoh's anger, who led Elijah to a near-death mountaintop experience while Jezebel was trying to kill him, who led Paul into prison, who led Civil Rights protesters into beatings and jail, and who led Jesus to the cross?

Gilmore got carried away with his rhymes. He paired "deepest gloom" with "where Eden's bowers bloom." Oh my. But there we have it. Adam and Eve were the holiest people ever, free to delight in all the delicacies of God's Garden. Yet they let themselves be led into disaster, to one of the blooming bowers, the one forbidden tree. Genesis 3 exposes the human flaw we all suffer: We have an itch to be like God, to be God.

How do we discern God's leading? God asks us to do things that are hard, that require courage, sacrifice, and an unflagging zeal no matter the cost. God leads us into the troubles of the world, precisely where Jesus walked every day. God leads us into the dark. We reach for God's hand. It feels not so much comforting as firm, maybe a bit dirty or bloody: Jesus' hand stretched out for our salvation.

Dietrich Bonhoeffer suggested that most of us prefer our own goodness to doing God's will.[6] But doesn't God want us to be good? If we dare to sing "He Leadeth Me," we dare to realize that God doesn't ask us to behave or stay out of trouble. Congressman John Lewis always said we should get into some "good trouble."

I wonder if he knew Bonhoeffer's thought that our goodness can actually block us from God's will. It's not about keeping our hands clean. It's about getting them dirty for God in the real world to work for change on God's good earth. Being led in this way really is a "blessed thought." Indeed, "and when my task on earth is done," I want to have stuck closely behind Jesus for days and years, having stumbled and gotten scraped up and bruised countless times. We start now. "His faithful follower I would be."

Merciful and Mighty

Hymns Praising God

*T*he spiritual life, especially in Lent, begins not with me, my quest, my struggles, or my belief but in the greatness of God. J. B. Phillips wrote a popular book whose title summarizes our foundational error: *Your God Is Too Small.* If we shrink God down to functioning like our personal assistant, an energy drink, or a Santa Claus that leaves gifts behind now and then, we will forever be just as small as our vision of God. To grow and discover the expanse of the soul God desires for us, we first must let our minds be blown by how overwhelmingly expansive, holy, wise and mighty—and yet merciful and tender—God really is. Hymns carry us a long way toward this humble, joyful realization.

God in Three Persons

$\mathcal{T}$he hymn I remember liking to sing as a child, for some reason, was "Holy, Holy, Holy." Maybe the words were easy for me because they were repetitive! So many of our hymns and praise songs veer toward the touchy-feely, the warm intimacy with God—which is fine—but "Holy, Holy, Holy" isn't about our feelings (or even us!) at all. It's about God. This hymn expresses awe. Being in awe is the gift of worship you won't stumble upon anywhere else in your life.

The hymn clearly plays on the call of Isaiah the prophet (see Isaiah 6). "In the year that King Uzziah died." That is, in the thick of politics and history, Isaiah was in the Temple, and the room literally came to life (in his imagination? in a vision from God? or both?). "I saw the LORD sitting on the throne"—not Uzziah or his heir, or the Assyrian emperor, or the Egyptian Pharaoh. God rules!

Then the Temple's carved creatures (cherubim and seraphim) came to life and began flying around with smoke, shadows, light, and God's voice. Isaiah trembled, as we all must if we ponder the immense holiness, grandeur, and might of God's presence. Those creatures sang to God: "Holy, holy, holy is the LORD of hosts; the whole earth is full of his glory" (Isa. 6:3). When we sing this hymn, we join angelic creatures and saints in heaven glorifying God.

God is "holy." What is this holiness? Is it refraining from evil? That can't be hard for God. Rabbi Jonathan Sacks points out that, in the Bible, holiness is this: God, who was infinite and had no problems at all, created, making space for us and for big challenges.[1] Just as God pulled back to make space and time for us, so we pull back, rest, and make space and time for God. We realize our dependence upon God. We can be like God. We "take time to be holy," to get close to God and mirror God's heart, mind, and being. That doesn't mean that we strive to be holy enough that God will draw near. Rather we dare to draw near to God or to make space to notice God's nearness. As we praise and soak up that glorious holiness, we become holy. Singing it is a good start.

The thrice repeated "Holy" led later Christian theologians to reflect on God as Trinity: Father, Son, and Holy Spirit, a mystery but a reality. God is eternally a fellowship of three within God's own heart. Singing to that fellowship that is God creates fellowship among us and with them. The tune we sing is called "Nicaea," recalling the historic church council in the year 325 when theologians, bishops, and pastors firmed up what the Bible teaches and what we believe about God as Father, Son, and Holy Spirit.

Music itself, and this hymn in particular, can help us envision God as Trinity. Jeremy Begbie points out that if you play a single note, let's say the first one in this hymn, it fills the room, not in one place more than any other. Then the second "holy" is another note, which joins without crowding out the first note. And then the third "holy" is a third note. The three together form a chord. All three notes fill the room completely, and the beauty of the full chord is greater than even the single note. Isn't God—Father, Son, and Holy Spirit—like that?[2]

This same angelic hymn appears elsewhere in scripture. In Revelation 4, the creatures around God's throne sing "Holy, holy, holy!"—and we can be sure that the early Christians, persecuted and intimidated by Roman emperors, centurions, soldiers, and tax collectors, boldly and courageously sang these counter-cultural words, declaring their unflagging devotion to Christ their Lord rather than to Caesar, who only pretended to be Lord.

I love that we sing this "early in the morning." "All the Saints adore thee"—and so when we sing, we join our voices to St. Francis of Assisi, Mother Teresa, my grandparents, and a holy host of those who are with God, the cherubim, and the seraphim. This awe-inspiring, majestic, all-powerful God is "merciful and mighty." Notice the order. God's mercy is the main thing; God's might is only a tool God uses in his larger labor of mercy. God's true might *is* mercy. "Though the darkness hide thee." If God is hard to see, it is actually the very nature of God to be beyond comprehension. And if we sing, "All thy works shall praise thy name," perhaps we will see the trees, clouds, salamanders, mountains, grass, and people around us as evidence of God's creative wisdom and generosity.

Here I Am

$\mathcal{I}$saiah somehow recovers from being nearly annihilated by the shock and awe of God and the singing of "Holy, Holy, Holy." We can imagine he was dizzy with the overwhelming and direct presence of the holy—and a bit surprised that he had even survived. What can he do then but offer to do whatever God might ask? "Here I am, Lord." He doesn't say, "I'd like to volunteer some of my valuable time" or "I can donate my great skill." God is laughably uninterested in human ability. God needs only availability. Moses can't speak well. Jeremiah is too young. Mary has never been with a man. Isaiah isn't very holy. All we can say before the holy God is "Here I am."

When my denomination's new hymnal came out in 1989, resistance to the incorporation of new hymns faded when we realized how marvelous some of them were. Michael Card's "El Shaddai" and John Wimber's "Spirit Song" became instant favorites. I immediately found a new favorite in "Here I Am, Lord," which had been written just eight years earlier by thirty-one-year-old Dan Schutte for a friend's ordination.

Worship isn't spending an hour with God and then being done, with mission as an optional add-on. I have a pastor friend who ends each service by saying, "The worship has ended, now the service begins." If we get worship, if we get being in God's presence (like Isaiah did when he heard them singing "Holy, Holy, Holy"), then we offer ourselves and go out to be God's presence with and for others. And we do so with considerable passion and energy.

"Here I Am, Lord" begins by inviting us to sing God's words and mood. This is the way to be one with God! God hears the people's cries and asks, "Who will bear my light to them?" and "Whom shall I send?" Isaiah, who was the only person in the Temple, must have wondered, "Who, me?" But then the God who can animate a stone temple and set seraphim and cherubim dancing around in the air can use Isaiah, me, you, anybody. And such a God, when so palpably present, is hard to turn down.

What is the rousing reply we're drawn into making with Isaiah through this hymn? "Here I am, Lord . . . I have heard you calling in the night; I will go Lord . . . I will hold your people in my heart." Don't sing this unless you're seriously ready for your routine life and your accustomed ways to be interrupted. We hear the cries God hears; we hold God's people in our hearts—reminding me of how Bob Pierce (World Vision's founder) prays, "Let my heart be broken by the things that break the heart of God."[3] How counter-cultural! When people come upon pain, they avert their gaze, or they blame, pity, or get scared. Isaiah and our hymn suggest we embrace the pain and go, being God's light to others.

The words are lavish and suggestive. For the "poor and lame" there is to be a "feast" with "finest bread," not a cheap handout but something really good, the kind of thing we treat ourselves to. The hymn confesses we've developed "hearts of stone." But God will break that stone and fill us with "love alone."

The prophecies in the book of Isaiah pick up on this image one more time late in the book, back in chapter 65. God shifts the image: Instead of God's seeking us, God wishes to be sought. "I was ready . . . to be found by those who did not seek me. I said 'Here I am, here I am,' to a nation that did not call on my name. I held out my hands all day long to a rebellious people" (Isa. 65:1-2). This is fascinating. God yearns for us. When we sing "Here I Am, Lord," we might hear God's plaintive plea to us: "Here I am, here I am." Will we seek the Lord and let our hearts of stone be softened? Will we then go to spread a feast for the poor and to be God's light in the darkness, only to discover God was there before us?

Day 6

Our God, Our Help

*A*fter a teenaged Isaac Watts complained to his father about lackluster music in church, his dad said, "Give us something better, young man."⁴ Young Isaac did, writing one hymn per week to the enthusiastic reception of the congregation. Imagine sitting in a pew, sight-reading the local boy's hymn of the week, and finding works such as "When I Survey the Wondrous Cross," "Joy to the World," "Jesus Shall Reign," and the hymn we're looking at just now, "O God, Our Help in Ages Past."

Fast forward three centuries. Lots of people laugh and identify with comedian Eddie Izzard's lampooning of this grand old hymn: "There's something phenomenally dreary about Christian singing"—and he illustrates by singing "O God, Our Help" like a dirge. Noting that people of color sing more enthusiastically, as their joyous music is "borne out of kidnapping, imprisonment, slavery, murder," he muses that white people with power and money are "the only people that can sing *hallelujah* without feeling." He envisions God listening and with a sigh asking, "What on earth is that?"⁵

Indeed, it is impossible to envision "O God, Our Help" being sung to a snappy pop tune. The content, like the St. Anne tune we've known forever, is stately, lofty, monumental. It feels like a monument because it is. The hymn ponders what has been around forever, since "ages past," "before the hills in order stood, or earth received her frame." The unfathomable expanse of time stretching before us, now dwarfing the ticking clock today: "A thousand ages, in thy sight, are like an evening gone." Time flies. And we don't kill time. Time kills us. Yet the hymn doesn't mash you down into insignificance. Instead, we small mortals are swept up into God's eternity, the unimaginably massive scope of God, and the endless stretch of time still to come.

Watts was reflecting on one of the Bible's most profound Psalms, the 90th, which is attributed to Moses, the old man of the mountain himself. Psalm 90 is more of a meditation than a prayer. And how fitting that Moses, who lived well past 100, is linked to this rumination on our frailty and how transient even the best among us really is. On the brink of entering the Promised Land, Moses died. Even he was denied total fulfillment in this life. Martin Luther King Jr., in his final sermon, hauntingly alluded to that moment, declaring "I've seen the promised land. I may not get there with you."[6] Reinhold Niebuhr was right: "Nothing that is worth doing can be achieved in our lifetime; therefore we must be saved by hope."[7]

Hope is the gift of Psalm 90, and of "O God, Our Help in Ages Past." Yes, our lives are blindingly brief; Shakespeare's Macbeth named it as a "brief candle," our life "a walking shadow, a poor player that struts and frets his hour upon the stage."[8] But wasn't Macbeth unduly cynical? Does time signify nothing? Lent invites us not to avert our gaze from how fleeting life is. This isn't cause for despair, but for the discovery of true joy. Watts's original hymn began, not "O God," but "Our God, our help." We don't possess or box God in, yet God is ours. We belong. We have a family kinship with the God beyond all space and time. This is our hope, that a

God so all-encompassing, so enduring, so unchanging, is still "our help," "our defense."

This is true even, and especially in the hour of death. "Time like an ever-rolling stream bears all its sons away." Newer hymnals, trying to be inclusive, tinker with this, leaving us with "bears all who breathe away." But they're not breathing anymore! When we aren't breathing any more, and this moment is coming all too soon, God will still be God, still our help and defense, "our eternal home." Notice those final words. It's not that God provides some eternal home. Far better: God, God's own self, *is* our eternal home.

Could it be that this is the case even for the thinly religious, the less than devout, those who believe in other manifestations of God, or don't think twice about God? This elegant hymn was sung at the funeral for Winston Churchill, who'd lived almost as long as Moses, and achieved much glory in this world. He was not a pious person; he jokingly said he wasn't exactly one of the pillars of the church, but one of its "buttresses," supporting from the outside.[9] Sufficient is God's arm to gather even these into that eternal home.

Day 7

How Great Thou Art

$\mathcal{W}$hen I was a boy, my mother tuned in to the Billy Graham crusades on television. I don't recall much of what Graham said, but I was always struck and moved (as much as a little kid can be "moved") by George Beverly Shea singing "How Great Thou Art." It's a great hymn, reminding us just how great God is.

We often underestimate God's grandeur. We whittle God down to size, to an assistant, a power boost, a doctor's helper, or a rescuer in times of trial. God is not so small, utilizable, or dispensable; God is not a helpful extra. Idolatry is when we shrink God down to a tool or machine, a badge to stick on our political ideology, or a hideout from the challenges of the world.

We will never exaggerate when we speak of God's amazing greatness. Our most spectacular, eloquent words, songs, and actions will be embarrassingly modest, falling far short of how great God is. When I think of this hymn and of God's greatness, I recall the times I've heard it sung in faraway places and in different languages. Once, with a group of pilgrims at the Jordan River, we peered across the place where Jesus may well have been baptized and admired a group of Korean Christians singing a stirring rendition of "How Great Thou Art." They'd come from the other side of the globe to the place where Jesus showed us how great God really is, and there they were, singing enthusiastically. We echoed their rendition, singing back in English. God's greatness echoed for just a marvelous moment.

God is so great, encompassing all people, everywhere and always, that we are summoned by that greatness not to settle back into our easy chair. If God is great, then we are set free to be courageous for God. We are required to be bold for God. We cannot help but labor for those God cares about—if this God really is as great as we sing.

The hymn literally directs our attention heavenward. "I see the stars." Of course, pollution and urban ambient light make it so we can't see as many stars as our grandparents, St. Francis, or Jesus did. Aristotle believed stars left a trail of music as they travelled through the heavens.[10] Dante spoke of God as "the love that moves the stars." Indeed, God "determines the number of the stars; he gives to all of them their names" (Ps. 147:4).

Years ago, my friend Ralph called me late one night asking me to bring my children to his house quickly. He had a big telescope set up in the driveway, and we all squinted into it and saw moons orbiting Saturn. Ralph always knew what would appear and when. This predictability and awe-inspiring order and grandeur made him feel, as he repeatedly told me, "at home in the universe."

Those stars seem so gentle adorning the night sky. We forget they are massive fireballs; if you were to get within a few thousand miles you'd be incinerated. Nature is like that: loveliness and terror, beauty and peril. "I hear the rolling thunder." We see a lightning flash. The sound rumbles in a few seconds later. I count in my head, calculating how far away the electrical arc actually is. Ancient people cowered in fear of their gods, imagining them tossing down thunderbolts of wrath. Israel's God wasn't moody like that. And yet the world has its built-in risks. Thunder, stars, just being alive:

it's dangerous out there. Something in the edgy precariousness of it all elicits even greater praise in our hearts.

This hymn recognizes that God's greatness is embodied in Christ, who sacrificed everything—even his own life—to liberate us from sin and death. And he's not done; he's not a figure in the religious past. "When Christ shall come . . . and take me home, what joy shall fill my heart." This thrills me every time we sing it.

And what will heaven be like? Will it just mean having fun with people we like? Hardly. It will be something far grander: "Then I shall bow in humble adoration, and there proclaim, my God, how great thou art!" We will need an eternity to try to tell God how awed we are, how grateful we are, how humbled and ennobled we are to be God's people, and to delight in the gift of dwelling—forever!—in God's presence.

And Take Me Home

*H*ow Great Thou Art" is a dramatic movement from praising God in the wonders of creation—from the sublime grandeur of mountain peaks to the singing of birds, from thunder up in the clouds to a brook meandering through the woods, from the starry host to a gentle breeze—to the purpose and turning point of it all, the cross of Christ.

All this sets the stage for the climactic vision of the fourth stanza, which doesn't fantasize about when we go to heaven but rather "when Christ shall come," which is the Bible's vision. The overwhelmed, giddy, awed exclamation of all creation will be a "shout of acclamation," reminding us of Psalm 47, where the Israelites in the Temple literally shouted as the ark of the covenant was hoisted and carried to the altar.

Then our hearts are opened by the phrase "and take me home." Where is home for you? Are you at home now? The question is not "Are you at your address?" It is "Are you home?" St. Augustine famously began his life's narrative by summarizing his story and ours: "You made us with yourself as our goal, and our heart is restless until it rests in you."[11] We are all always looking for something, someone, or someplace, like that prodigal son in Jesus' best story (see Luke 15:11-32).

We know this restless sense of yearning for home but never quite settling in. Carl Sandburg wrote that Abraham Lincoln never felt at home in any of the thirty-one rooms of the White House.[12] Anne Tyler's novel *Dinner at the Homesick Restaurant* tells the story of Ezra Tull inheriting Mrs. Scarlatti's restaurant, where he'd worked. He renamed it the "Homesick Restaurant" and got rid of the menu. Customers would name food they were homesick for, and cook would make it.

God seems to have fashioned us with a hankering for home and also with the gnawing sensation that we're never quite there. It might feel like nostalgia for some hazy yesteryear (that maybe wasn't really as marvelous as you recall). But what is nostalgia anyhow? The word derives from Greek roots meaning an ache for home. Can you remember such a place? You want it, you crave it, you're driven by the quest to figure out just where and what it is.

We get surprising glimpses now and then. Dolly Parton had a hit with "My Tennessee Mountain Home" and then built a huge theme park around a replica of her childhood home. She calls this the "golden thread that keeps me tied to Eternity."[13] Tourists flock to it by the thousands. They're having fun, but many report being touched by some deep memory and yearning. What's downright shocking is how popular her song is in countries like Kenya, England, and Lebanon, where Appalachian culture could not be more alien. It's because of that home-shaped hole in the heart of every person. God is calling us "softly and tenderly" to "Come home."

For me, the home in my heart wasn't a house where my nuclear family lived. We were an Air Force family that moved a lot, and my parents were at war with one another. So home for me was my grandparents' home in a sleepy, middle-of-nowhere town called

Oakboro. My memory of it is expansive, as if it were a huge mansion. But I was a bit stunned by its actual size when I went back to visit years after my grandparents had died. It was just a small bungalow of no architectural distinction. Nostalgia, or my God-given ache for home, had expanded the place to fit the space in my soul. I wanted to go back and be welcomed home as I'd been as a wee one.

I stood in the yard for a few minutes and wondered what it had been like when my dad returned there from World War II. Back in those days of no immediate communication, families could just wait and hope for good news. So many young boys were killed in action, but my dad, in his early twenties, returned and was embraced with shouts and tears. It was probably a lot like the homecoming Jesus pictured when that prodigal finally found his way down the road to home.

Doesn't "How Great Thou Art" invite us to dream of such a day when Christ will bring us home? The plot of the gospel is that God in Christ made his home among us so that he might then bring us home to God. The promise, the hope, the assurance is that the elusive home we've known and yet have always sought so earnestly is waiting for us. We'll get there; we're headed that way even now. So let's exhale, sigh, and even rest a little on the journey. Then what will rush into that empty place where we've just breathed out our frustrating seeking? "What joy shall fill my heart."

One Little Word
Shall Fell Him

$\mathcal{M}$y daughter Sarah and I were poking around in the Augustinian monastery in Erfurt, Germany, where Martin Luther figured out who he was and what God was asking of him, when we stumbled upon a tour group. Their guide was explaining that we were in the very room where Luther and the monks worshiped every day. It was stone, medieval, with live acoustics: a lovely place. Without any warning or anyone saying anything at all, the tour group began to sing "A Mighty Fortress Is Our God" with much emotion and tears. When they were done, I found out they were recently retired Lutheran pastors who'd dreamed all their lives of coming to this place and singing this hymn, their hymn.

Luther sparked the Reformation, wrote voluminously, translated the Bible into German—and wrote hymns. He understood music's power to heal, forge bonds, and encourage. He wrote that hymn-singing is "a fair and lovely gift of God . . . I have no use for cranks who despise music . . . Music drives away the Devil and makes people gay. They forget wrath, arrogance and the like."[14]

During a season of profound depression and discouragement, Luther wrote his most famous hymn, "A Mighty Fortress Is Our God," which picks up on themes in Psalm 46. It's not that God makes everything smooth and easy. But God is "a bulwark . . . our helper amid the flood of mortal ills prevailing."

Luther understood that life isn't just human beings doing good (or not). There is a cosmic battle going on all the time; invisible but real forces of evil are arrayed against the good. "Our ancient foe doth seek to work us woe, his craft and power are great." Indeed, evil is "armed with cruel hate." Sound pertinent to our world?

We don't defeat evil by trying hard or thinking right thoughts. "Did we in our own strength confide, our striving would be losing." And why can we be bold and confident? We have "the right man on our side . . . Dost ask who that may be? Christ Jesus, it is he . . . He must win the battle." Ours is to follow, join, and be caught up in the wake of what he is doing.

And so "We will not fear." There is plenty to fear. Not all fear is bad. Is a truck bearing down on you crossing the road? Then you should be afraid and move quickly. But much fear is irrational and overwhelming. This is intriguing: After Paul wrote "Have no anxiety," he added, "In everything by prayer and supplication with thanksgiving let your requests be made known to God" (Phil. 4:6, rsv). I used to make requests of God, and then I would give thanks if God did what I wanted—assuming I remembered to do so. But we must begin in gratitude. It is from that space that we ask for God's help.

What does that have to do with fear and anxiety? Psychiatrist Martin Seligman reports on studies that show that writing five thank-you notes a day or jotting down lists of things you're grateful for will reduce your anxiety and depression scores by a noticeable percentage.[15] I find when I am a thankful person, when I am in the act of expressing gratitude, I do not feel anxious. If we look back with gratitude, then we naturally look forward with hope. It is the antithesis of looking back with guilt or regret, which leaves you stuck looking forward with nothing but anxiety and fear.

This is not to minimize all there is to fear: mortality, losing a loved one, winding up alone, finances. What is worst of all? "The Prince of darkness grim." I love that it adds "grim." For Luther, the devil was so very real that he threw things at him and hollered. "His doom is sure. One little word shall fell him"—which may be my favorite moment in the hymn. What is that one little word? *Jesus? Grace?* Some believe Luther was thinking of the angel in Revelation 14 who encountered the devil's spewing of hate-filled words, blasphemies, and falsehoods. The angel simply responded, "Liar." There are so many lies out there: *You aren't enough. You don't belong. Money is everything. Power is everything. It's all up to you.* These are all lies that elicit fear and anxiety. The Christian relies on just a word. Maybe it's "Liar!" Maybe it's "Grace." Maybe it's simply "Jesus."

A Place of Quiet Rest

*W*hat is God's greatest achievement, the truest indication of the magnificence of God? It is that God—instead of being merely omnipotent (merely omnipotent?), omniscient, omnipresent, infinite, ineffable, and transcendent—is primarily tender, present, closer than the breath you just drew, feeling the beating of your heart, loving you personally more than you love yourself or anybody else.

One of the hymns my grandmother sang while doing her chores or cooking dinner was "Near to the Heart of God." Picture this: The God who had the power to create the universe, with galaxies and nebulae and black holes, not to mention the peaks of the Alps and the depths of the oceans, was on intimate terms with a short, aging woman from nowhere in particular. No matter the circumstance, she knew what the Bible's poet declared: "For me it is good to be near God" (Ps. 73:28).

"There is a place of quiet rest, near to the heart of God." Where is this place? In my heart, of course. But you probably also need an actual place of quiet rest. Jesus spoke of shutting the door of your closet and praying in there (see Matthew 6:6). When I was a boy, there was a huge rock in the woods behind our house. I used to climb to the top and just sit there daydreaming. I wasn't trying to practice sabbath or being still and knowing God was God (see

Psalm 46:10). But I believe God was luring me there, preparing me to be someone who would always yearn for a place of quiet rest near to the heart of God.

We all yearn for quiet, and yet we harbor a fear of silence. The quiet feels like loneliness. I can't dodge my self-doubts or worries when it's quiet. The hymn says this quiet rest is "a place where sin cannot molest." Yet that's exactly what I'm afraid of! The darkness might jump me in the quiet. But in reality it jumps me when I'm rushing around.

The spiritual life is learning the delights of solitude, which isn't loneliness but resting in and with God. It's not taking a nap or getting away for a vacation. It's not doing nothing; it is being. You probably need a dedicated place. You certainly will need to shut off your gadgets. The single greatest peril to the dream of a prayerful life is that we are always available for a text, a call, or an email. But if you're always available, then you're never available to God or to other people. We must find the way to visit Sabbath, to be still and know that God is God, to take a seat in the term Abraham Heschel used to describe the Sabbath: a "cathedral" of time.[16]

"Hold us who wait before thee near to the heart of God." How often does the Bible invite us to wait on the Lord? We don't like to wait in line, in a waiting room, or for a diagnosis. It's the loss of control. And yet, the one we are waiting on is our Lord. So instead of flitting away we ask him to hold us. Please. We can be held. We can trust.

My mother-in-law used to speak of her morning prayer as her "lap time," imagining that she would curl up in her heavenly Father's lap, not to ask for favors, but simply to be, to feel the love.

Brian Doyle recalled when his sons would fall asleep on their pew during worship. He thought of this as "sheer simple mammalian affection, the wordless pleasure of leaning against someone you love and trust."[17] After they were grown and had leaned away from parents and church, he asked them to sit with him once more in worship as he was dying of cancer. Those little boys were now strong, and in his weakened state he was the one leaning on them.

This leaning, this wordless pleasure, reminds us of our life with God. It is one of the ways God is close to us. I leaned more than once on my grandmother, the one who sang "There is a place of quiet rest, near to the heart of God." Our hearts beating together, as close to God's heart as you can get on this earth. "A place of comfort sweet . . . a place where all is joy and peace, near to the heart of God."

Beautiful Savior

Hymns About Jesus

*T*he Christian life isn't about faith or spiritual feelings or being good. It's about Jesus. The Gospels tell us about people who either dropped everything and traipsed off after this man Jesus or scoffed and conspired to get rid of him. Lent isn't a season to try to agree with Jesus' ideas or to behave in ways that might make him proud of us. Christianity is about following a real person. The more clearly we see, hear, and understand him, the closer we can stick to him—which is the only reason to bother with something like Lent or the rest of the Christian year.

Fairest Lord Jesus

*H*ow intriguing that most of us have little snatches of memory from early childhood, not a continuous story but a moment here or there that has stuck somehow. I was maybe four or five when my mother took me with her to a white cinder-block church near our home in Savannah, where my dad was serving in the Air Force. We were picking up my older sister, Jann, who had been dropped off for children's choir practice. They weren't done yet, so we sat in the hall. From behind the closed door I heard little girls singing "Fairest Lord Jesus," first in unison and then in harmony. It struck me as so beautiful that it was unforgettable.

God gave humans the capacity to make beautiful sounds with our voices. And the wonder of harmony is amazing: We have to work together, we need one another, and the shared effort is glorious. We humans can make beautiful sounds together, and usually we do so in response to beauty, praising beauty. If you hear or sing something beautiful, some composer likely made something beautiful in response to something beautiful. And then we are ourselves beautiful in the singing of it.

This is worth pondering, especially since we live in a world of so much ugliness. There's suffering and meanness. People hurt one another, and they hurt themselves. Dostoyevsky wrote that "the world will be saved by beauty."[1] What else could possibly redeem ugliness?

"Fairest Lord Jesus" simply notices and then extols the beauty of Jesus. He must have been immensely and mystically attractive, since people dropped everything to follow him. They risked and lost their lives for him, so great was their devotion to him. So beautiful was his life, and especially his suffering and death, that artists, painters, sculptors, composers, and poets have created and created, trying to recapture that beauty. Rembrandt captured the light and shadow of the adoration of the shepherds at his birth. Michelangelo sculpted Mary holding her crucified son and painted a handsome Jesus calmly presiding over the Last Judgment. Caravaggio picked up on Michelangelo's creative finger from the Sistine Chapel and used it to show Jesus' calling of Matthew, and he also graphically portrayed Thomas poking a finger into the wound in Jesus' side. Bach's *St. Matthew Passion* and *St. John Passion* rhapsodized at length over the glory of Jesus' story of salvation.

The crucified Jesus is the most peculiar beauty. What could be more horrific, agonizing, and unjust? It is the kind of thing from which you avert your gaze or simply shudder. And yet that moment has inspired the most beautiful artistic achievements. Matthias Grünewald, Salvador Dali, Georges Rouault: The list goes on and on of those who grasped how beautiful Jesus was precisely in the moment of his humiliation and his piercing and gruesome pain. The fourteenth-century mystic Julian of Norwich, after receiving beautiful visions of the beautiful Jesus, wrote that everything else was now ugly to her except the crucified Jesus.[2]

This hymn is very old and is sung to an old Silesian tune from centuries ago. A myth arose that the Crusaders sang this hymn as they marched off to war. I hope and pray this is false! If it is true, it would only prove the Crusaders were blind to the beauty of the Savior of which they sang. The Crusades are our constant reminder that religious zeal can easily run amok and attach itself to ugly causes that are not of God.

Nature's beauty is itself a reflection of Jesus' own beauty. Thomas Aquinas reminded us that God wove beauty into the world to reflect God's own beauty.[3] Jesus will "make the woeful heart to sing" no matter how we think of him: in his mother's womb, as an infant in the manger, as a healer, as a teacher, as one who touched the untouchable, in agony on the cross, rising triumphantly from the tomb, or tenderly forgiving and sending. The antidote to sorrow isn't having a bunch of fun; it is looking to Jesus. The antidote to despair is praise. For us, we see the Beautiful Savior at our Lord's table.

You Have Come to the Lakeshore

$\mathcal{T}$he first time I heard and sang "Lord, You Have Come to the Lakeshore," I was in Stuart Auditorium looking out over Lake Junaluska, a Methodist gathering place in the mountains of North Carolina. It reminded me of the times I've visited the shore of Galilee, and I felt transported back in time to that moment when Jesus first came to the lakeshore:

> Jesus was walking by the Sea of Galilee. He saw two brothers, Simon and Andrew, casting their nets into the lake, for they were fishermen. Jesus said "Come, follow me, and I will make you fishers of other people." And at once they left their nets and followed him (Matt. 4:18-20, AP).

The composer, Cesáreo Gabaráin, was a Spanish priest who started writing music for humble people in a more folksy style after the Roman Catholic Church's reforms at the Second Vatican Council (1965). His hymn tune (Pescador de Hombres, "Fisher of Men") has a waltzing, lilting feel, mimicking the feeling of being in a boat rocked to and fro by the gentle waves.

Water has such astonishing beauty. A landscape photo or painting is more lovely if a river runs through it. John O'Donohue notices, "Water stirs something very deep and ancient in the human heart. Our eyes and hearts follow its rhythm as if the flow of water were the mirror where time becomes obliquely visible. The image of water can hold such longing."[4]

Why are we so drawn to water? Is it because we began our lives in the water of our mother's womb? Is it that our bodies are mostly water? Water quenches thirst, washes us clean, and is simply beautiful to behold. And it is not entirely safe. How many of the Gospel stories feature the disciples being terrified on that very lake? Doesn't the water symbolize our inevitable humility, defying our grossly overrated ability to manage things?

God has provided us bodies of water to keep us humble but also on an unending quest for more. Isaac Newton summed up all his knowledge: "I seem to have been only like a boy playing on the sea-shore, and diverting myself in now and then finding a smoother pebble or a prettier shell than ordinary, while the great ocean of truth lay all undiscovered before me."[5]

It's intriguing to me that Jesus' first encounters with those who would become his closest friends and most zealous followers took place not just by the water but also in the workplace. Jesus came— and comes—to the places where people work. You don't need to try to haul your faith into the workplace. Jesus is already there, showing up for work before you arrive—and you can't get rid of him there either. The love, grace, call, and challenge are all around you, if you (like Simon and Andrew) have the ears to hear.

Gabaráin's hymn claims that Jesus showed up at work looking "neither for wealthy nor wise ones, neither gold nor weapons." Rather Jesus was seeking "humble followers." Yes, "Lord, you know my possessions . . . my nets and labor . . . With your eyes you have searched me, and while smiling have spoken my name."

How lovely. Jesus knows you, your work, your stuff. Imagine him with you, looking at you, into you, not past you, and he smiles and speaks your name.

It turns out that this Jesus who gifts you with presence and love also needs you. In the third stanza we sing, "You need my hands, full of caring through my labors to give others rest, and constant love that keeps on loving." Another Spanish Catholic, St. Teresa of Ávila, is reported to have said, "Yours are the hands of Christ. . . . Yours are the hands with which he is to bless now." Look at your hands before work, during work, after work, and ask how you might bless others, how you might be God's constant love through whatever you do.

Beyond the Sacred Page

*N*estled a few yards above the northwestern shore of the Sea of Galilee at place called Tabgha is a lovely church marking the traditional spot where Jesus multiplied the loaves and fishes to feed five thousand people. An ancient mosaic on the floor depicts the fish and the bread. When we step outside and stand near the water, we envision Jesus breaking the bread over and over again to feed the hungry people.

When we think of the Bible as being "inspired," we tend to think of God's influence in its writing, or perhaps we think of inspired people having shared their inspired thoughts with us. Inspiration might also be the way God's Spirit grabs you for a swift journey back in time and to another place until—*voilá!*—you are there by the sea with all the rest. Jesus gives the bread, not to them but to you and to us.

"Break thou the bread of life, dear Lord, to me, as thou didst break the loaves beside the sea." Jesus breaks the bread, and you get enough. Our being there with him is mediated through the biblical story. The Bible passage becomes itself the bread, broken open, perhaps the way Jesus broke open the meaning of the scriptures for the disciples in Emmaus (see Luke 24:13-35). We pray for the mysterious, healing truths of the Bible story to be cracked open so we can see, taste, understand, and be filled and changed.

The drama in John 6 takes us on a long journey to understand what Jesus was and is about. When Jesus multiplied the bread for the hungry crowd, their bellies were filled, and they were giddy with enthusiasm. This must be the Messiah! Just as God provided manna in the wilderness (see Exodus 16), so this great man has made even more bread unfold out here in this wilderness. There must have been shouts of approval and joy.

But then Jesus shifted the topic from bread to the bread of life—as in the will of God, as in not living by bread alone but by every word from the mouth of the Lord, as in following him (see John 6:35-40). Grumbling and murmuring—like that of the Israelites of old—ensued. Jesus, not easing up for a second, pressed further: "The bread that I will give for the life of the world is my flesh" (John 6:51). Now he's talking about suffering and crucifixion. Not surprisingly, the flustered crowd fled for home. Only a handful of the thousands who got the free lunch were left standing around.

"Break thou the bread of life." We're asking Jesus to teach us. We're also asking Jesus to die for us. Break the bread: You, the bread of life, be broken for us. Jesus understood. Weeks later, he held the Passover loaf in his hands, tore it, and shuddered as he saw in it what would become of his body. Break thou the bread of life, dear Lord.

No wonder our hymn zigs and zags off toward another passage of scripture: "As a deer longs for flowing streams, so my soul longs for you, O God" (Ps. 42:1). "My spirit pants for thee." The thought of our Lord breaking himself for us takes my breath away. I gasp, I sigh, I breathe in deeply and exhale. This is the one I'm thirsty for, hungry for, flat out desperate for. I'll find him now—at the table in my church.

And I'll find him in the scriptures. Let there be no confusion: The Bible isn't God. We don't believe in the Bible. "Beyond the sacred page, I seek thee, Lord." That sacred page is our way to the face of God, to the bread of life. When I delve into and through the Bible, when I find myself transported back into its live moments and the bread is broken, everything changes. "Then shall all bondage cease, all fetters fall." That's another story or two in that bread of life book. Paul's fetters were broken in Philippi, although he didn't run off (see Acts 16:16-40). As Lazarus stumbled out of his grave, Jesus said, "Unbind him, and let him go" (John 11:44). Jesus was sealed in a tomb with guards, but he broke free, cracking the world and all its assumptions wide open.

God's extravagance is absurd. It's like manna, a little, just enough. But then it's plenty, way more than enough. When Jesus broke the bread beside the sea, he got carried away. Thousands ate plenty and had basketfuls left over. "Break thou the bread of life," we pray—and we'd best brace ourselves. An abundance of bread, truth, holiness, love, mercy, and hope are about to burst forth from the broken place.

What a Friend We Have

*M*iriam Cohen's book *Will I Have a Friend?* envisions an anxious child's first day at school. It's a good grown-up question too: "Will I have a friend?" Does it help to sing "What a friend we have in Jesus"? Despite the corny, repetitive rhymes (bear, prayer, bear, anywhere, share, prayer, there) that led hymn expert Albert Edward Bailey to say, "It is not good poetry . . . It is what might be called doggerel,"[6] the hymn is much beloved, evoking a sense of warmth and familiarity. But the image of Jesus as friend is even more profound than we might imagine.

At the Last Supper, Jesus tells the disciples, "No longer do I call you servants . . . but I have called you friends" (John 15:15, rsv). Up to this moment, Jesus has given them good cause to think of him as Lord, God, Word incarnate, Light of the World, Savior. But then this utterly magnificent, inspiring, divine one invites them to see him as a friend. What could he mean?

For us, a "friend" might be someone we have fun with, someone who likes what we like, someone like us, someone easy to be around. But such friendships can be thin. We hold back from going very deep, not wanting to risk disagreement. So we stick to chatter about food or sports. Or we find our way into little enclaves of people who agree with us, echo chambers for our biases that feed our narcissism. Isn't it true that spending time only with people like us will make us ignorant and arrogant?

Ancient philosophers like Socrates defined a "friend" as someone who helps you to become good and wise. Aristotle wrote that the opposite of a friend is a flatterer. Christian thinkers from St. Augustine to Søren Kierkegaard thought of friends as those who help you to love God, and whom you help to love God. Paul Wadell reminds us that "Friendship is the crucible of the moral life."[7] You become the people you befriend. It's formative. If Jesus is your friend, you become like him, prayerful, generous, and ready to lose everything to do the will of your Father. You will begin touching untouchables and seeing through fake religiosity.

The secret to young Methodism's vitality was that John Wesley insisted that people get organized into small groups to share in the quest for holiness. We need friends who care about and dare to cultivate wisdom and holiness, who hold one another accountable for progress toward Jesus our shared friend. Jesus explained why he would be calling the disciples friends: "For all that I have heard from my Father I have made known to you" (John 15:15, RSV). Friends share God's knowledge. They are learners, pushing one another on to more expansive understandings of the heart of God.

Aelred of Rievaulx, a twelfth-century Cistercian monk, said to his friend Ivo, "Here we are, you and I, and I hope a third, Christ, is in our midst."[8] What would it be like if Christ were in your friendships? Whom are we called to befriend if Jesus, befriender of a scandalously diverse grab bag of people, is our friend? G. K. Chesterton wryly declared that St. Francis "seems to have liked everybody, but especially those whom others disliked him for liking."[9] He sounds like a friend of Jesus.

When Jesus is our friend, we celebrate differences with friends. You disagree? Instead of drifting away, friends of Jesus labor toward reconciliation, knowing that Jesus didn't run off when we were difficult, wrong, or less than faithful. Martin Luther King's insight, "Love is the only force capable of transforming an enemy into a friend,"[10] makes me wonder how many friends I've missed out on.

What are the habits of friendship? Friends eat together. We dine with Jesus at the Lord's Supper. And at all our meals with friends. We dare to be vulnerable. Brené Brown reminds us that friendship never happens without the courageous risk of vulnerability, candor, and sharing. "What a privilege to carry everything to God in prayer," and what a privilege to carry everything to a friend down here over dinner. Jesus "knows our every weakness" (see Hebrews 4:15), inspiring us toward friendships here that know weakness and love.

Friendship is encouragement. "We should never be discouraged." The tenderest way Jesus our friend alleviates our discouragement is when a friend encourages us. And friendship is sacrifice. Jesus, the best friend ever, said, "No one has greater love than this, to lay down one's life for one's friends" (John 15:13)—and then he went out into the night to be arrested, tried, and crucified—for us, his friends. What is Lent, if not being drawn into a deeper friendship with Jesus?

Jesus, Lover

*J*esus is my friend. But Jesus, _Lover_? We think of Jesus as friend, Lord, Son of God, prophet, teacher, Savior, and even our brother. But do we think of Jesus as a lover? In _The Last Temptation of Christ_, Nikos Kazantzakis cast Jesus as Mary Magdalene's lover to the consternation of many Christians. Yet, when Charles Wesley wrote "Jesus, Lover of My Soul," he was using a constant and provocative image that dated from the early church and persisted through the Middle Ages.

Medieval people developed a deeply emotional sense of Jesus as one with whom you would be intimate. They meant spiritually, of course, and yet with palpable physical sensations. St. Teresa of Ávila was sculpted by Bernini as being in spiritual ecstasy, her posture and facial expression identical to what one would expect from a woman experiencing sexual climax. John Donne's famous sonnet pleads:

Batter my heart, three-person'd God . . .

Except you enthrall me, never shall be free,

Nor ever chaste, except you ravish me.

St. Thérèse of Lisieux, late in the nineteenth century, spoke of her experience of Jesus:

Ah, how sweet was that first kiss of Jesus! It was a kiss of
love, I felt that I was loved, and I said: "I love you, and I
give myself to you forever!"

Frequently and with no embarrassment, Thérèse kissed her cruci-
fix right on the face. She grew more eager to die, praying that God
might take her without delay into his eternal embrace so that "I
may be able to tell you of my love eternally face to face."[11]

Bernard of Clairvaux called the Holy Spirit "the kiss of God"
and was perhaps the greatest of all preachers and commentators on
The Song of Songs from the Old Testament, a little book that sur-
prises people who do not expect to find erotic love poetry in their
Bibles. Over the years Jewish rabbis and Christian theologians have
found the inclusion of the Song of Songs in the Bible puzzling too,
and most of them have concluded that the only reasonable theological explanation for it is that the lovers in the book represent the
Lord and his people.

Maybe what lovers experience is a window into what might
unfold with Jesus. Is physical pleasure somehow like the pleasure
one might have in Jesus? Is our romantic pleasure even a mystic
taste of intimacy with God? If Jesus is "lover," might Christians
learn to talk in healthier ways about sexuality? We tend to twist
this fertile field into a battlefield, or we just hush and don't mention it. But intimacy isn't something we do in hiding from God.
Romantic relationships and faith relationships are related.

How might serious prayer be like sex within a loving relationship? There is losing yourself, shedding inhibitions, a total expo-
sure of yourself, holding the other gently, trying to give pleasure
as much as receive it, a lost sense of the passing of time—and so
much trust and even a kind of awkwardness. Mercy and tenderness are required. Words fail you, and yet words must be attached.

The lovers in the Song of Songs rhapsodize about the loveliness of the beloved. Perhaps brushing up on how to speak words of adoration to those we love will help us praise God more fully. Or, as we practice our praise of God, we will sharpen our ability to praise our beloved. Hyperbole and exaggeration are in order—although it's not exaggeration at all when you're caught up in love.

Reportedly, Charles Wesley composed this hymn as a result of a harrowing experience aboard a ship that nearly sank in the ocean right after his and his brother John's abysmal failures as missionaries to Georgia. Terrified, dejected, and seasick, he turned to Jesus as lover. "Let me to thy bosom fly." If you were in some hopeless peril, if your life were hanging in the balance, whom would you want by your side, intertwined in embraces? The hero you hope will rescue you? Or the beloved who knows you best, whom you know best, and with whom you have shared precious intimacy?

Cleft for Me

$\mathcal{J}$esus invites us into an intimacy with him without losing the jaw-dropping awe. The are two held closely together in the old hymn, "Rock of Ages." Roger Scruton, a philosopher of beauty, contrasts the serene beauty of a green meadow with a "wind-blown mountain crag [where] we experience the vastness, the power, the threatening majesty of the natural world, and feel our own littleness in the face of it."[12] This we call "sublime," which doesn't mean "super-beautiful" but rather a beauty that humbles and even frightens a little. It's thrilling and inspiring; it underlines our finitude and our frailty.

Isn't God like such a sublime mountain crag? We are in awe. We tremble a little and wonder if it's safe. We can't just jog to the top. We feel small and yet drawn into the wonder. How perfect that so many mountain scenes figure prominently in God's revealing God's mind and grandeur to us.

Jesus' most famous sermon was on "the Mount." Jesus was on a mountaintop when he suddenly shone like the sun and was joined by Moses and Elijah, mountain men themselves. Moses had ascended Mount Sinai, conversed with God for weeks, and then come down with divine laws, his face glowing. The whole book of Deuteronomy takes place on Mount Pisgah. God spoke to Elijah in the silence on Mount Horeb. Solomon built his temple on Mount

Zion. Abraham carried his young son up on Mount Moriah, fearing the worst. And Jesus was crucified "on a hill far away."

Think of huge rocks you've seen in person or in photos: El Capitan, Kilimanjaro, Gibraltar, the munros in Scotland, the Matterhorn, or Sugarloaf. God is old, massive, substantial, enduring anything and everything, breathtaking, not easily mastered. How tender then, that when the Bible tries to comfort us, it speaks of God being a "refuge," a "fortress," or a "hiding place," inviting us to envision ourselves up high on the mountain that is God, but in a safe cave, a sheltered niche in the rock, near God, secure in the presence of God the sublime. "You who live in the shelter of the Most High, who abide in the shadow of the Almighty, will say to the LORD, 'My refuge and my fortress; my God, in whom I trust'" (Ps. 91:1-2).

Many Psalms describe birds and other creatures nesting in clefts in mountains as illustrations of God's protection during literal or figurative storms. On Mount Sinai Moses asks to see God's glory. God's reply is merciful and sublime: "You cannot see my face. . . . There is a place by me where you shall stand on the rock; and while my glory passes by I will put you in a cleft of the rock, and I will cover you with my hand until I have passed by; then I will take away my hand, and you shall see my back" (Exod. 33:20-23). Rock of ages, cleft for Moses.

St. Francis loved to climb mountains and sleep in caves. When he observed rocks jutting out, inaccessible ravines, or gravity-defying stone formations, he believed (as did many medieval people) that all those formations came to be on Good Friday. Right after the Temple curtain was torn, "the earth shook, and the rocks were split" (Matt. 27:51). The impact rippled all over the earth, so when Francis napped on a boulder or grabbed a little stone outcropping to climb higher, he felt very close to Jesus on the cross. When he felt he was under assault by the devil, he would crawl into a crevice on a mountainside to hide. Not surprisingly, when medieval people would gaze on the wounds in Christ's body in the crucifixes that hung in their churches, they thought of his wounds as nooks in the sides of Jesus their "rock" where the deeply spiritual could flee for solace.

Augustus Toplady wrote this marvelous hymn in England in 1776, just as Revolution was starting in America. He borrowed the idea from one of John Wesley's hymns,[13] which is odd because he had engaged in a testy theological feud with Wesley, appalled that Wesley overrated human ability to be holy and to achieve God's will. Every phrase of his hymn emphasizes how utterly lost and incapable we are, but it is no counsel of despair. Rather it shows an intense trust in divine goodness, mercy, and power.

"Nothing in my hand . . . I come to thee helpless." Anyone battling addiction knows that only when you acknowledge utter helplessness can there be any hope for healing. The same holds for spiritual hollowness or the dream of salvation. The hymn recalls that the largest cleft in that rock of Jesus' body resulted from the soldier's piercing lance. Water and blood poured out; Toplady's hymn calls it the "double cure for sin." Indeed, Jesus' blood, shed for us, and the waters of baptism cleanse and save us.

Little Ones to Him Belong

*O*ne of the greatest theologians of the twentieth century, Karl Barth, whose *Church Dogmatics* explaining the Christian faith ran to thirteen thick volumes, was once asked if he could offer a succinct summary of his theology. He said, "Jesus loves me, this I know, for the Bible tells me so." Generations of children have memorized this little song and have sung it with zeal and joy. Jesus not only loved those guys back then, but Jesus loves me here and now.

What is this love? Is it like a parent's love for a child? Lovers for one another? I love a good story, good wine, and good music. I love my friend who died last year. What is Jesus' love for me like? And even more important, if Jesus loves me, how do I love him back? Do I love him back?

Jesus cooked breakfast for the disciples and then asked Peter, "Do you love me?" (see John 21:15-19). Jesus loves me, this I know, and I also know he asks me across time and space, "Do you love me?" I want to say yes. I want to live into that yes. But what does that mean?

The hymn provides a tantalizing clue. "Little ones to him belong." When you see children singing this, you think, *Yes, these little ones belong to Jesus.* But what did Jesus, in "the Bible tells me so," say about little ones? Jesus welcomed them when others thought they should be shushed; he spoke to grown-ups and said,

"Unless you change and become like children, you will never enter the kingdom of heaven" (Matt. 18:3). He can't have meant that you must become cute, quarrelsome with siblings, silly, or pouty. Children are dependent and they know it. Children haven't foreclosed on dreams or what the future holds. Children trust. Children notice dandelions and bugs. Children have more questions than answers. Children can't keep secrets. Their calendars aren't full. They aren't in a big hurry. They daydream.

Jesus' last sermon spoke of care for people who are hungry, thirsty, alone, poorly clothed, sick, and imprisoned. He said that the way we have treated one of "the least of these" or "these little ones" is how we have treated Jesus himself. Little ones to him belong: not just our precious children in our cherub choir but the little ones, the least, the ones the world dismisses as being too insignificant to bother with. The time-tested formula for growth in the spiritual life includes connecting with the least, those in need.

And that doesn't mean just dropping off worn-out, unwanted items. My children poke fun at me when they recall the "sweet potato caper." After walking out to drive to church, I remembered it was the day of the food drive. I opened our pantry, quickly grabbed a couple of cans of sweet potatoes, and took them to the drop-off. I hate sweet potatoes. As I've done it to one of the least of these, I've done it to Jesus? Here, Jesus, take these sweet potatoes off my hands?

Quite a few times, people in my churches have brought me a ham at Thanksgiving or Christmas and told me to get it to a needy person. On my terrible days, I thank them. On my better days, I've said, "Take it to the needy person's home yourself." On my best days, I've suggested they invite the needy person to their home and enjoy the ham together. Jesus ate with strangers. The little ones, like diminutive Zacchaeus, belonged to him, so he broke bread in the home of the stranger, and nothing was ever the same.

If we ponder the mercy and miracle that Jesus loved us when we'd made ourselves strangers to him, then loving him in return by loving the stranger is a simple reflex of mercy. Besides, if we only hang around with people who are like us, we become ignorant and arrogant. Spiritual growth is overcoming both. Jesus spoke of clothing the naked—and there are so many ways to share in this work through clothing closets and sewing groups. If you sew, your life's mission might be to wind up like Tabitha (known as Dorcas, see Acts 9:36-43): When she died, the poor women of Joppa wept bitterly and showed Peter the garments she had made for them.

Mother Teresa explained all the worldwide labors of the Sisters of Charity as nothing more (or less) than simple love for Jesus in the person of his little ones. The Bible tells us it is so. Little ones to him and to us—Jesus' body now on earth—belong.

Prone to Wander

HYMNS OF FORGIVENESS

*S*in, Lent's primal theme that nobody really likes to think much about, isn't self-recrimination (*I'm a bad person* or *I made a mess of things*) or a nagging guilt for having done wrong. Sin is visible when we see ourselves in the light of Jesus' life—the life upon which this past week's hymns have reflected. The gap between our lives and Jesus' words, actions, and being is the space we desperately want bridged; this is the healing we need but cannot manufacture, and this is the great grief of our soul. Could a hymn bring a cure? Could a hymn even restore us to what God made us to be?

Raise Mine Ebenezer

$\mathcal{I}$t is so lovely when a hymn bridges the gulf between human brokenness and the divine presence. "Come, Thou Fount of Every Blessing" succeeds marvelously, partly due to its tune and harmonies. Without the words it feels cheerful, soaring upward and then settling back down to earth. Yet when we sing of "streams of mercy, never ceasing," we acknowledge the never ceasing need for that mercy. When we ask God to "tune my heart to sing thy grace," we fully own how our hearts get out of tune; some dissonant racket clutters the soundtrack of our lives. This tune, called "Nettleton," itself tunes our heart to lift our voices in "some melodious sonnet" with "songs of loudest praise."

How do we get out of tune in the first place? Guitar and piano strings need regular attention. Pressure, time, temperature, and humidity slowly and imperceptibly pull an E string down toward an E-flat or even a D, never to a higher pitch but always sagging lower. Life's pressures, the passing of time, the heat of the day, and our tears can all be depressive, bringing us down. In God's mercy, the truth of God's grace wrenches upward what has sagged, returning our hearts to their proper place: the mood of praise for the "fount of every blessing."

What is a blessing anyhow? We get confused, like a rickety out-of-tune piano, thinking that a "blessing" is something we wish we had: nice house, cute knickknacks, sumptuous food, a new car, stellar health, or a growing family with a golden retriever at our feet. Our hymn knows better. The blessing is God's mercy, which extends to us from the height of "the mount of thy redeeming love." Which mount is this? God's love gave Moses the commandments on Mount Sinai. Jesus taught from a mount above Galilee. The Jordan river flows mightily from the melting snows of Mount Hermon. Solomon's temple was built on Mount Zion. But it's the mount of Calvary where, "to rescue me from danger," Jesus "interposed his precious blood."

Because of the unlimited scope of this blessing, *the* blessing, we needn't shrink from the truth about ourselves. Jesus' precious blood exposes and embraces our broken realities. My heart is a "wandering heart." I have made myself a "stranger" to God, myself, and others. Indeed, we are all "prone to wander." In case you missed it, this proneness is repeated: "Prone to wander, Lord, I feel it, prone to leave the God I love." Like the sheep that are so often referenced in the Bible, we nibble a little here, then there, losing sight of the shepherd, dumbly wandering away from our protector, the one who cares and can lead us to life and back into the fold.

I hear an echo of Isaac Watts's paraphrase of Psalm 23: "My shepherd . . . you bring my wand'ring spirit back . . . Oh, may your house be my abode . . . Here would I find a settled rest . . . no more a stranger, nor a guest, but like a child at home."[1] What could be more tender and more blessed than a lost child returning home? And staying home. Many Americans trumpet "freedom" as God's great blessing. But we're not so free as we think. We find ourselves shackled to sin and mortality. We would prefer to be tethered to our caring Lord: "Let thy goodness, like a fetter, bind my wandering heart to thee."

There is one last mystery to explore. Stanza two begins "Here I raise mine Ebenezer." In the seventh chapter of First Samuel, the Philistines were on the verge of annihilating the Israelites. But, with help from Samuel's faithful leadership, God delivered the people. In gratitude and to mark the memory forever, Samuel erected a large stone monument and named it "Ebenezer," which in Hebrew means "stone of help." Think of stones of help. In Israel and many other places, stone walls keep sheep close to home. The so-called "Wailing Wall" in Jerusalem is an impressive array of huge stones where people pray, inserting little paper prayers.

Near where I live, the Catholic basilica at Belmont Abbey has an Ebenezer-like baptismal font. A large stone that once functioned as a trading block for the marketing of enslaved persons in antebellum America was re-carved and made into the font, bearing this inscription: "Upon this rock, men once were sold into slavery. Now upon this rock, through the waters of baptism, men become free children of God." The Ebenezer font is the fount of every blessing.

Ten Thousand Charms

*W*inston Churchill, fumbling for words and sensing a need to apologize for being old when he was courting Clementine, parroted something he'd heard in church, but he made a funny addition: "We are all worms. But I do believe that I am a glowworm."[2] The psalm Jesus prayed from the cross includes the confession, "I am a worm" (Ps. 22:6). In our culture, with its sunny views of the virtues of positive thinking and self-regard, the hymn "Come, Ye Sinners, Poor and Needy" is an uncomfortably countercultural expression of what it's like for us worms.

The hymn invites us to name that we are not only "poor and needy" but also "sick and sore." We may not readily resonate with the idea that we are "lost and ruined by the fall." Yet what is the deep truth of the human condition? What do I see behind my eyes when I do more than glance in the mirror, when I'm lying awake in the middle of the night, when I have mucked things up? If I linger long enough to feel the darkness in my soul and the dysfunction in my relationships, and especially if I weigh how very thin my relationship with God actually is, how frail my spirituality is, how flawed my goodness is, and how utterly lacking I am in holiness, then I feel sick. I feel sore places.

Archbishop Oscar Romero said that the hard mission entrusted to the church is to uproot sins from history, politics, and the economy: "No one wants to have a sore spot touched, and therefore a society with so many sores twitches when someone has the courage to touch it and say: 'You have to treat that. You have to get rid of that. Believe in Christ. Be converted.'"[3]

What we desperately need is some miraculous healing. Gritting your teeth and trying to do and be better won't cut it, as the hymn gently reminds us: "If you tarry till you're better, you will never come at all" and "Let not conscience make you linger, nor of fitness fondly dream." Indeed, God's only requirement is "to feel your need of him." When don't we feel such need?

After this diagnosis that is enough to make you shiver, it's easier to comprehend the hymn's appeal to those of us who are "thirsty": "Come, and welcome, God's free bounty glorify" is a deliberate echo of the prophet's stunning, hopeful words to the forlorn exiles in Babylon who had concluded that God had given up on them (see Isaiah 55:1). Then stanza three embraces the "weary" and "heavy laden." We're invited to hear Jesus speaking once upon a time but also to us now: "Come to me, all who labor and are heavy laden, and I will give you rest" (Matt. 11:28, RSV).

The mystery is in the refrain: "O there are ten thousand charms." We've just sung how Jesus will embrace us when we go to him. Are the ten thousand charms in his arms? Are they some vast array of blessings or an overflow of mercy? Maybe. But the music reverts to the minor chord that opens the hymn; is it something more sinister?

When Joseph Hart wrote this hymn in the eighteenth century, the word "charm" meant some kind of incantation, a magical spell, or an amulet or talisman you might carry. The clear connotation of *charm* was of something alluring, beguiling, and bewitching. So yes, "I will arise and go to Jesus." But there are thousands of allurements, and the world working its multiple spells on me to yank me away from Jesus' arms. It is a warning, a humbled sigh of the ongoing struggle. It's akin to the second stanza of "O Jesus, I Have Promised": "O let me feel thee near me! The world is ever near; I see the sights that dazzle, the tempting sounds I hear," not to mention the third stanza's "storms of passion" and "the murmurs of self-will."

Hart knew this all too well. Until he was about thirty years old, he had strived to be good, holy, and of service to God. But then he lapsed into what he called his "libertine" phase. For a dozen years he lived as he wished, abandoning worship and any shred of doing good. After his reconversion, he regretted those years but understood intimately the relentless pursuit of the world to reclaim those lost to the Lord. "O there are ten thousand charms."

To Rid My Soul of One Dark Blot

$\mathcal{I}$n one of the evangelist Tony Campolo's funny set pieces, he would speak of a revival service where the pastor would issue an altar call, inviting people to come during the singing of "Just as I Am." Indeed, after a few stanzas, one of the brethren would come, "just as I am," kneel and pray fervently—and then when the service had ended, he would head back home (as Tony put it), "just as he was."

Is it that God accepts you "just the way you are"? Or is God's business to take the ramshackle you and convert you into something you should or could be? Is the gospel about the recovery of the real you that has gotten caked over with phony stuff? Is the conversion settling back (or forward) into the pure you, the child within, the image of God never fully expunged by the world or the mess you've made of things? Paul Tillich famously described being "struck by grace" like this:

> A wave of light breaks into our darkness, and it is as though a voice were saying: "You are accepted . . . accepted by that which is greater than you . . . Do not try to do anything now; perhaps later you will do much . . . Simply accept the fact that you are accepted!"[4]

"Just as I am, without one plea, but that thy blood was shed for me." The theological theory of the Atonement—the idea that Jesus died in my place—lurks behind this. What can we make of this, especially during Lent? The idea that God was really angry about human sin and vented that anger on his own son instead of on us is nonsensical and downright blasphemous if you think about it. What a petty deity this would be to require blood vengeance.

Yet, that Jesus' blood was "shed for me" is the ultimate secret to Christianity. It is the scandal of the Cross. God became human, was pierced, and died—but it wasn't simply a tragedy, the sad story of a good man who died wrongly. His blood somehow was an expiation for sin. As Jesus bled on the cross, God's love for all people was being poured out. Mercy overflowed from his beautiful body to bring healing to people who didn't understand, weren't all that holy, and thought of God as their grand benefactor in the sky instead of as their brother in suffering and death.

God loves you and all of us—the soldiers gambling for his clothing, the thief on the cross next to him, and the person who has broken your trust—that much. Just as I am, I ponder this marvel. Just as I am, I soak in the glory of this humbling truth. And perhaps, if I go deeper, I might pray not only to admire Jesus' suffering but to share in it, to love as he loved and to bear the cost with him.

The hymn echoes well the turmoil most of us feel in the soul: "tossed about, with many a conflict, many a doubt, fightings and fears within, without." For me the most intriguing line in the hymn is "To rid my soul of one dark blot." Do I have just one dark blot? Or is there a lot of regrettable ink splattered on my soul? Maybe it's a theological Rorschach test. I inspect the blot that is in me. The blot that *is* me. Do I have problems? Am I a problem?

Yes to both. I have sins. Plural. But sin is a condition. It's me, all of us actually, distanced infinitely from God, thinking that I can manage on my own. I can fix my own problems. It's really all about me. I am the center of the universe. I must justify myself. I must be good enough. I must *be* enough. To this "one dark blot," Jesus responds by inviting us to ponder that "one thing is needful" (Luke 10:42, rsv). It's not that a thousand fixes are required for my thousand messes. I am one problem. Jesus is the one blotter-outer. I come as I am to Jesus, who "wilt welcome, pardon, cleanse."

Then it adds "relieve." Is being out of trouble with God my relief? Or is it having the massive weight of life apart from grace lifted from me? So many of us live like Atlas, the Greek demigod who carries the weight of the world on his shoulders. But God's got it. Or we carry the burden of thinking we are to judge others. God's got that too. You're relieved of that awful burden. And so you can live freely, more lightly, and in the great joy of God's good mercy.

You have to get up out of your easy chair and come. The clincher in this hymn is what worked in the altar call: "I come." And it's repeated if you're hesitant: "I come." Come. Come to Jesus. Just as you are. You'll never be the same.

Day 19

All Loves Excelling

$\mathcal{S}$in only matters because of the immensity of the divine love. The distance between ourselves and God's holiness is bridged by that love, and it comes entirely from God's side. Thankfully, the "joy of heaven" is "to earth come down," as sung in the first phrase in what could be the best of Charles Wesley's 6,500 hymns, "Love Divine, All Loves Excelling." Walter Brueggemann calls it "a well-nigh perfect hymn."[5]

If there's anything perfect in the hymn, it is its realization of the perfection of God's love. We might think we know what love is, and then we infer that God that must be like that. But God's love is overwhelmingly and delightfully so much greater, more marvelous, and more extensive than all the love we might imagine woven together. Yet it's accessible; it's personal and as small as a hug or a young child nestled in your lap: "Joy of heaven to earth come down." Indeed, God made a "humble dwelling" down here in Bethlehem when Jesus was born. Or as the ancient Christian hymn in Philippians 2 puts it, "Though he was in the form of God, emptied himself, born in human likeness" (AP).

For the hymn, that joy come down to the "humble dwelling" isn't a once-upon-a-time story of old. "Fix in us thy humble dwelling." It is a miracle: God is born once more in me and in you.

What if we walked around all day thinking *God has fixed in me his humble dwelling*?

"Breathe, O breathe thy loving Spirit" into us. In a way, God is already doing this. While you've been reading, you've inhaled more than a dozen times. That is God's breath, God's Spirit rhythmically giving you life and love—and it's involuntary! You weren't even trying or asking. God's grace just comes. We recall when God breathed into humanity the breath of life (see Genesis 2:7) and that moment after Easter when Jesus met the disciples and breathed on them (see John 20:19-22).

"Take away our bent to sinning." Judaism teaches that all of us have a *yetzer ha'ra* in the soul, an inclination to sin. Christianity says we are fallen creatures, mired in sin and shackled by self and the world. We can't just grit our teeth and not sin. We can only ask God to take it away: "Set our hearts at liberty." Americans, for example, boast of their freedom, even as they doggedly embrace their stuckness in the culture, the anxiety, the trendiness, and the rancor of the world. As Galatians 5 shows us, God sets bound people free—not so we can do as we wish but so we can be fruitful for God.

"Alpha and Omega" is our God (as extolled in Revelation 21:6)—the first and last letters of the Greek alphabet serving as a metaphor for the totality of God's grace, the all-encompassing range of God's boundless love. What's most profound in the hymn and about this beginning and ending is rarely noticed: "End of faith as its beginning." God is, as we know, the "end," the goal, the object, and the purpose of faith. But God is also the beginning of faith. Faith isn't merely how we access God. Faith is itself a gift—maybe God's greatest gift (along with breath, of course). If you have faith, you can't pat yourself on the back for being so clever as to believe. Belief itself comes from God despite you, despite your unfaith!

The last stanza looks forward to the final crescendo and glorious conclusion of God's long work since Creation: "Finish then thy new creation." What will that kingdom of God—that eternal life—be like for us? We ask now for God to begin to bring to fruition God's eternal purpose for us: "Pure and spotless let us be." I'm not, but I want to be.

But God's not done with me just yet. In the meantime, when I ponder God's love and determined labor to finish me and all creation, my mind is boggled and my heart is moved. I might just find myself "lost in wonder, love, and praise."

A Thousand Tongues

Charles Wesley certainly got lost in praise, and his hymns capture the way we finally understand our sin from God's viewpoint when we are swept up in praise. "O For a Thousand Tongues to Sing" is the first hymn in Methodist hymnals and is almost the anthem of Methodism. It originally stretched to nineteen stanzas—as if Wesley just couldn't contain his wonder, love, and praise.

He wrote this hymn on the anniversary of his conversion. It was reportedly inspired by a chance remark by a Moravian missionary named Peter Böhler: "Had I a thousand tongues, I would praise Him with all of them."[6]

What do we think as we sing "O for a thousand tongues"? Frankly, the one tongue you have doesn't praise God very much. We are so utilitarian when it comes to God. What's God done for me lately? What do I fantasize God will do for me next?

St. Augustine distinguished between two Latin words for love.[7] *Uti* is love of use: I love something, not in and of itself, but because I use it for something else. I love money. I don't want to cuddle with it or frame it; I love it because I can use it to get other things I want. Then there's *frui*, the love of enjoyment, what I love . . . just because. I love chocolate, not because of what I get out of it. I just love it. I must have it.

We tend to love God with *uti*—I think I'll use God to get stuff I want—when God is seeking *frui* from us, simple adoration, what Wesley called "my great redeemer's praise, the glories of my God and King."

Praise, *frui* for God, is a gift we ask for: "Assist me to proclaim." Praise is also the fruit of long practice, an extended retraining of the soul. Praise isn't a mood but a disposition in your character. Rabbi Jonathan Sacks reminds us, "It would have been easy for God to create a billion computers programmed to sing His praises continually. But that would not be worship."[8]

Charles Wesley had been a bit of a dogged, computer-like adherent to Christianity. He'd never missed church. He was engaged in Bible study, disciplined prayer, and service to the poor. He was dedicated to small groups of mutual accountability. So his "conversion" wasn't as if he were a pagan one day and a believer the next. For Charles and his big brother John, the magic of 1738 was that the truths of the faith and the activities of holiness incumbent on the believer bored their way deep into their hearts. It got personal. Their deepest selves were stirred. "He sets the prisoner free." Churchy religiosity can be a kind of bondage. No wonder many congregations sing this hymn on Reformation Sunday.

John Wesley explained that he finally grasped that what Christ had done was done *pro me*, "for me." Not for me only, but most assuredly for me. This personalized "for me" is echoed in Charles's hymn: "His blood availed for me." He'd known about Jesus' sacrificial atonement on the cross and had preached it and composed hymns about it. But in the spring of 1738, it was as if a new person was birthed out of that old one. He'd been born into a Christian household. Now he was born again, with passion and assurance.

Böhler's (and Wesley's) wish for a thousand tongues, which is vivid hyperbole, is literally granted when we recall that we never praise God alone. I might be in a sanctuary with a few dozen others. But at that moment, dozens of dozens of others are praising in churches nearby. If we think of the churches across the globe and God's people throughout time, the numbers begin to stagger the mind. What do we sing at Christmas? "Sing, all ye citizens of heaven above." Saints and our own beloved, a countless host, join with us, even leading us in praise. They don't have that *uti/frui* dilemma we do. They just praise constantly and are filled with delight. Our praise is never a solo. We are part of Christ's universal Body that praises together.

It Is Well

$\mathcal{I}$f one thing sticks in the minds of seminarians after studying medieval church history, it is the quote from Julian of Norwich: "All shall be well, and all shall be well, and all manner of things shall be well."[9] Actually, those were words Jesus himself spoke to her. In the year 1373, she had a series of visions in which she saw the crucified Christ, who conversed with her. The "All shall be well" is the centerpiece of much profound theological exploration in her report of her visions.

It may seem a bit naïve to sum up the gospel as "All shall be well." This is the kind of trivial spirituality people love: that everything is good, life is sweet, and tomorrow will be a happy day. But Jesus said this to Julian as she wrestled with stark realities of suffering and sin. She lived in a small brick cell in the city of Norwich during the Great Plague of Europe. More than half the population of Norwich perished. The Hundred Years' War was simultaneously raging, and the worst schism in history was tearing the church asunder. In such a terrifying, insecure, bleak moment, Jesus told her, those who listened to her, and we who read her today, "All shall be well, all manner of things shall be well."

Part of me wants to argue with him or her. "Yes, but . . ." Yet seminarians remember those words, and they linger in my heart. Just hearing them defying muddy reality, despite the news of the world crumbling around us and our own personal losses and fears, brings inexplicable but certain comfort. I believe it. All really will be well. In the moment of hearing it, saying it, or singing it, I believe.

In 1873, exactly five hundred years after Julian's visions, Horatio Spafford wrote "It Is Well with My Soul." The backstory is stunning. Two years earlier, his four-year-old son had died of scarlet fever. Then Spafford sent his family to Europe aboard the steamship *Ville du Havre*, planning to join them later. Disaster struck. The ship sank, and 226 people were killed. Spafford's daughters were all killed. His wife, Anna, somehow survived and sent a telegram across the Atlantic to her husband, stating simply, "Saved alone."

He caught the next ship to Europe. Imagine that: Through most of human history, people did not enjoy instant communication or rapid travel. For days on end, he suffered alone in his anguish, trying to reach his wife. As he crossed the ocean, he stood on deck watching the waves—the immense water that had just a few days earlier engulfed his own children—and wrote "When sorrows, like sea billows roll." In the rocking of the waves on his boat, he felt the agony and grief he then offered to God in his hymn.

It is fascinating that Spafford contemplated his sin—and probably that of his wife and children—in that moment. We don't think much about sin, or we attribute it to wicked people we don't know or like. But Spafford knew his sin, his brokenness, his crushing distance from God—and in his grief he dared to notice that "Christ has regarded my helpless estate. . . . My sin, not in part but the whole, is nailed to the cross, and I bear it no more."

We have, through our sin, our fumbling spirituality, and our rebellion against God's ways, made a gulf between ourselves and God. Even in our most grievous moments, this sin lingers and needs healing. Maybe especially then. Did Spafford feel guilty because he'd not travelled with them? Did he feel like there was something he could have done?

But his hymn declares God's healing, the forgiveness that he didn't earn or achieve. It is simply God's most astonishing gift, given even to the heartbroken and devastated. God's presence in sorrow is huge, but it is not the end of the story. "And Lord, haste the day that my faith shall be sight"—that day when "the trump shall resound." Sailing across the ocean, crushed by grief, eager to embrace his wife in her unspeakable sorrow, he courageously dared to believe that God holds out a better day, a future of reunion, restoration, and redemption. All will be well. It is well with my soul.

Spafford travelled later to Israel and established there the American Colony, dedicated to the care for the needy and suffering in Jerusalem and neighboring Palestine. When we know that life is fragile, when we trust in God's good future, then this is the sort of thing we do when all is well.

It is well. Jesus says, "All shall be well." It is well even now.

Day 22

Feed Me Til I Want No More

*T*he Sinai Peninsula is a dry, barren, forbidding place. Imagine the Israelites, thousands of them, without a compass, army, food or water supply, wandering around out there for forty years. That wilderness wandering has become a parable of the Christian life, although a few days of spiritual dryness isn't quite as daunting as spending decades out on sandy, rocky terrain in soaring temperatures and with the occasional gnat and locust swarm.

"Guide me, O thou great Jehovah, pilgrim through this barren land" is a lovely and fitting prayer to God. We want guidance, which is more than general wisdom about doing the right thing. If you go on a wilderness trek, your guide is the one you stick close to. She warns you about dangers and knows where the shade and watering holes are. Guide me. I'm like a child, I'm weak in this spiritual life, so "hold me with thy powerful hand." Imagine walking through your days with God's firm hand in yours, God's secure grip, comforting and guiding. Over here. This way now. Careful.

Lest we forget, as God guided the Israelites, they murmured and kept planning to bolt and return to Egypt. But God fed them manna, a blessing of immense mercy in response to their bitter complaints against Moses (and God!). We would expect sin to elicit God's rage, but it seems to stir God's mercy. As we sing these words, are we really any more pious or full of faith than they were?

The hymn picks up on other images from Exodus and Numbers, like the fountain (see Exodus 17:1-7) and the fire and cloud that gave direction by day and night (see Exodus 13:21). Not to mention Israel's arrival at their longed-for destination, crossing safely onto Canaan's side: "When I tread the verge of Jordan."

So many slave spirituals picked up on this imagery. "Deep river, my home is over Jordan" and "I am bound for the land of Canaan" were thinly veiled codes for hoping to cross over the Mason-Dixon line or to make it to Canada. Of course, that "verge of Jordan" also implies the end of life, instilling hope. President James Garfield, nearing death, brightened and then wept as his wife sang this hymn to him; and it was sung at Princess Diana's funeral.[10]

Perhaps more than any other hymn, this one could keep someone with a Bible concordance busy. The main focus seems to be the wilderness journey, but the hymn also quotes and alludes to a broad variety of texts: Numbers 20:2-13; Deuteronomy 8:15; Joshua 3; Psalm 78:52; John 4:14; 1 Corinthians 10:4; 2 Timothy 1:10; Hebrews 11:13; Revelation 22:1-2 and others. William Williams, who composed the hymn in his native Welsh, was one of those Christians who are so very deeply immersed in scripture that phrases fall effortlessly from their minds, as naturally as breathing comes to the rest of us.

Yet so many hymn writers miss the point in their excesses of exuberance. We have, for example, "Are Ye Able said the Master, to be crucified with me? . . . Yea, the sturdy dreamers answered, to the death we follow thee. Lord, we are able." When Jesus asked the disciples this very question, they too answered, "We are able" (Mark 10:39)—but the tragicomedy was that they most certainly were not able. Peter denied him. The others fled.

"Guide Me, O Thou Great Jehovah" makes a similar blunder. Appealing twice to God as "bread of heaven" and alluding to the provision of the manna in the wilderness, the hymn prays "Feed me till I want no more" and then repeats it. Like a family at Thanksgiving, we imagine ourselves feasting until our bellies are about to pop. Lord, give me all I want, even more, until I'm totally full. But the manna wasn't a bountiful meal. It was barely enough to get by for a day. And it had to get old, same manna, day after day, for months, years, decades. They got a little, and surely hankered for a little more. God gave them not their fill but enough.

The geniuses of the early centuries of the church understood the virtues of hunger and dissatisfaction. While many people in wealthy modern countries feel that all desires must be satisfied, early Christians knew that emptiness, craving, and unfulfilled desire for God was the secret to the spiritual life.

We have a hunger to know God. We learn a bit about God, but instead of that quenching our thirst, it makes us even thirstier for more of God. Then we apprehend even more of God; we feast on greater knowledge of God—only to discover that we are even more hollow now, yearning for even more. God made us this way. The joy is in the pursuit, in the gnawing desire for more, rather than in any fantasy of being full or of having gotten what there is to receive.

Thy Presence My Light

Hymns of Vision

The life of faith is all about seeing. It is not just looking but seeing, understanding the reality of things beneath the surface. Maybe it is seeing in the dark. "The Lord sees not as we see" (1 Sam. 16:7, AP). Faith is "the conviction of things not seen" (Heb. 11:1)—but then they are seen by the eyes of faith. Jesus' favorite miracle seemed to be healing the blind; there's something in this about those who thought they could see but couldn't really. Lent is a season of focus, a time for putting on the corrective lenses of the gospel.

Still Be My Vision

*H*ymns help us hear and see what God hears and sees. Who wrote "Be Thou My Vision" and why? Sometimes it's attributed to St. Patrick, the courageous fifth-century missionary to the Irish. Or maybe it was the writer St. Dallán Forgaill in the sixth century. It's been covered by lots of musicians, including Van Morrison. What thoughts have flitted through the minds and hearts of millions as they've sung this over the centuries?

My optometrist checks my vision and prescribes corrective lenses. He can explain why my vision is trending a certain way. Our hymn asks for a peculiar vision—that the Lord will not merely help or correct my vision but rather "Be thou my vision, O Lord." You be my eyes.

On the road to Damascus (see Acts 9), Paul experienced a transformative vision of Jesus. After a short stint of blindness, he recovered his sight. But he never saw anything the way he had previously. "From now on, therefore, we regard no one from a human point of view" (2 Cor. 5:16). We see ourselves, others, every situation, and all creation through the lens that is Jesus' life, cross, and resurrection. Our bodies aren't gangly, unwieldy things but temples of God's Spirit. There is beauty in the picturesque but also in aspects of God's creation that nobody thinks to photograph. Hope for reconciliation shines in the ugliest conflicts. Other people are divine image bearers.

Don't thoughts just happen? Don't they just pop into your head? Yes, but we have choices about what to think and what not to think. Reading scripture, singing hymns, worshipping, study, and service are a years-long tutorial in what and how to think. The goal? "Thou my best thought." Late in her life, Dorothy Day told how she once started to write a memoir but discovered she had no need to do that: "I just sat there and thought of our Lord, and his visit to us all those centuries ago, and I said to myself that my great luck was to have had Him on my mind for so long in my life!"[1]

Maybe that's how you turn out if your constant prayer is "Be thou my wisdom." We know smart, successful people. But who is wise? Henry David Thoreau mocked Harvard for teaching "all the branches [of knowledge], but none of the roots."[2] Wisdom is deep underground, not just lying around on the surface. We hear thin, pithy sayings pretending to be wise: "Time is money." "You get what you pay for." "When the going gets tough, the tough get going." "Life is short, play hard." "Bloom where you are planted." These are too trivial to be true; they are too insubstantial. Thoreau, who went to live in the woods in pursuit of wisdom, noted how technological advances are merely "improved means to unimproved ends."[3]

Wisdom thinks about the end, the purpose of life. Wisdom is serenity and patience. Wisdom must be cultivated and won over the length of life. Wisdom treasures what is old and has survived for a reason. Wisdom is born out of the cauldron of experience: hard times, grief, sacrifice. You can't just pick up an idea and suddenly become wise, the way you crack open a fortune cookie. You live it, wait on it, test it, let it seep up from the good earth through the soles of your feet. You become one with God, who is Wisdom.

The way to wisdom is "I ever with thee and thou with me, Lord . . . with thee one." Sam Wells suggested that the most important theological word in the Bible is *with*.[4] God is with us. This is a constant theme in our best hymns. That's what the psalmist sought after suffering much: "Nevertheless I am continually with you . . . There is nothing on earth that I desire other than you . . . For me it is good to be near God" (Ps. 73:23-28).

We stick close to God in prayer, immersion in scripture, holy conversation, and being with those in need. We never forget the quirkiness and scandal of divine wisdom. Paul wrote to the sophisticated, philosophically proud Corinthians that "the message about the cross is foolishness" and that God "will destroy the wisdom of the wise." "God's foolishness is wiser than human wisdom" precisely because "God chose what is foolish in the world to shame the wise" (see 1 Corinthians 1:18-27). Signs that this foolish wisdom has been cultivated in us are contentment, gratitude, and forgiveness. Our values are not defined by the world: "Riches I heed not, nor man's empty praise." The hymn itself pulls us into the very soul of God. What joy it is to sing that God is "heart of my own heart." The heart of my heart is the heart of God—which is the way to "reach heaven's joys."

Day 23

Thou Traveler Unknown

$\mathcal{T}$he art of seeing what God sees, and seeing as God sees, is doing so in the dark. Spirituality is a kind of night vision. Consider the unusual hymn "Come, O Thou Traveler Unknown." Very few hymns focus on a single story in the Bible. Charles Wesley must have spent a lot of time ruminating on the story of Jacob wrestling in the dark of night with a stranger (see Genesis 32:24-32).

Estranged from his brother for decades and with a troubled marriage, Jacob is alone, anxious, and on the run, evidently thrashing up against the limits of existence. He can't even get a good night's sleep. Terror of all terrors, he's tackled by . . . well, it's too dark to see. Is it a robber? Is it Esau? An angel? God? The ambiguity is the reality for Jacob—although the implication is that God is somehow mysteriously in the thick of this life-threatening assault.

Wesley's surprising insight is that he imagines Jacob actually inviting the perilous encounter: "Come, O thou traveler." Come. Bring it on. Jacob never shrinks from trouble and instigates plenty of it himself. He's a fighter, someone who relishes conflict. The biblical narrative indicates that God seems to enjoy it as well. What odd religions are Judaism and Christianity! We argue with God. We can do combat with the Almighty. God allows this. God welcomes this. God seems to want relentless, ferocious openness, honesty, and grappling from us.

A "traveler unknown" arrives in Jacob's camp. Who are the strange travelers in our world? Rabbi Jonathan Sacks sees God as revealing deep truths to us through the stranger, inviting the Jews to fight for the stranger since they have been strangers themselves:

> If you are human, so is he. If he is less than human, so are you. You must fight the hatred in your heart . . . Though they are not in your image, says God, they are nonetheless in Mine. There is only one reply strong enough to answer the question: Why should I not hate the stranger? Because the stranger is me.[5]

Indeed, Wesley's hymn presses the traveler: "Tell me if thy name is Love." God is in the stranger. Love is in the surprise encounter in the dark. God is with Jacob—by being against him and by wrestling with him.

In Wesley's hymn, Jacob doesn't try to escape: "With thee all night I mean to stay, and wrestle till the break of day." Does Wesley's hymn help us see what may be implied in Genesis 32? Jacob has chutzpah, a cockiness that dares to fight anybody, including God. He even fights God to something of a draw! And he isn't merely a survivor. As always, Jacob's getting something to take home: "I will not let you go, unless you bless me" (Gen. 32:26). He had stolen the blessing from his brother, and now he insists on another blessing. It's a model for prayer: We grapple with God; then we grab hold of God and won't let go until we get the blessing.

The bout is so intense that Jacob limps away from the scene. He is wounded, marked by the encounter. Contemplating Jacob, Sacks speaks of "honorable scars."[6] In Graham Greene's novel, *The End of the Affair*, a woman notices what used to be a wound on her lover's shoulder, and contemplates the advancing wrinkles in his face:

> I thought of lines life had put on his face as personal as a line of his writing: I thought of a new scar on his shoulder that wouldn't have been there if once he hadn't tried to protect another man's body from a falling wall . . . The scar was part of his character . . . and I knew I wanted that scar to exist through all eternity.[7]

Jacob is scarred; he limps, and his wound is the badge of honor from having engaged mightily with the Almighty.

Jesus had scars after Easter, scars he earned when he gave life to all of us, scars not blotted out by the resurrection (see John 20:27). Frederick Buechner envisioned this when he preached on Jacob limping away from his contest with God: "Remember Jesus of Nazareth, staggering on broken feet out of the tomb toward the Resurrection, bearing on his body the proud insignia of the defeat which is victory, the magnificent defeat of the human soul at the hands of God."[8]

Genesis 32 isn't about Jesus. Or maybe it is when seen through the eyes of faith. Wesley's hymn imagines an inquiry into the name of this nocturnal stranger, guessing that it's Love—with a capital L—and finally, and delightfully concluding, "Tis Love! Thou diedst for me."

And everybody else.

Everyone Born

*H*ymns extol God's goodness and bind the individual's soul to God. Hymns also can have an impact on society, on us as people together, and on the church's work out in the world. When the earliest Christians sang "Christ is Lord," it was a protest against the Roman Empire's claim that Caesar was lord. Slave spirituals were codes: "O Canaan, I am bound for Canaan" was biblical, but it was also a dream of escape to Canada! "We Shall Overcome" lifted sagging spirits during the Civil Rights movement. Even the revival of "God Bless America" after 9/11 revealed the power of a song to galvanize hope.

Given the disturbing debates within churches over issues like same-gender marriage, race, or immigration, it's not surprising that new music has emerged. In "All Are Welcome" we sing "Let us build a house where love can dwell and all can safely live, a place where saints and children tell how hearts learn to forgive. Here the love of Christ shall end divisions . . . All are welcome in this place." It's never enough just to sing "All are welcome," any more than it is for a church to stick a welcome sign in the front yard. We press on to ask who might not feel welcomed and why, and we feel restless ourselves until it really is *all* who are welcome.

Another lovely song achieving hymn status is "For Everyone Born." The gospel isn't just for some subset of humanity—those who are like us or politically correct or good patriots or straight. John Wesley sparked the Methodist revival by preaching "prevenient grace," which is God's loving and empowering regard for all who have accomplished just one thing: being born. The church's task isn't to pass judgment, condemn, or hunker down behind our secure walls. We dream of becoming a safe place for everyone. For that to happen, we have to get busy doing what Jesus told us to do: creating justice, discovering and spreading joy, and making peace instead of division. The hymn says this is God's joy too! "God will delight when we are creators of justice and joy."

"Everyone Born" is redundant, isn't it? Everyone born would be . . . everyone. You, other readers of this book, others singing the hymn, and people who would never do either were once a microscopic blob in mom's womb, dependent, fragile, a wonder. You were there before your mom was aware—but God knew. Psalm 139 probes this marvel of life *in utero*, the sheer miracle of being born, that mind-boggling transition from a dark, warm, aquatic zone out into the chill air and bright lights. You're born. Vulnerable. Asking only for tenderness and love.

This is why the Christian story is what it is. God thought, *I want them to know me, to love me.* Instead of coming down as a mighty warrior, God came as an infant, vulnerable, dependent, like everyone born. Jesus spoke mysteriously about being born again. That's not an emotional vibe at a revival service. It's the realization that we are like newborns: dependent for each breath, nourishment, and gentle handling, like everyone born. And so we sing and welcome and never rest until everyone born has what the hymn details: clean water, shelter, a safe place for growing, belonging, being heard, mercy—"a star overhead."

Dorothy Day taught us Christian table manners: "Let's all try to be poorer. My mother used to say, 'Everyone take less, and there will be room for one more.' There was always room for one more at our table."[9] And Jesus reminded us to invite to our dinner parties not those who can invite us in return but rather the poor, maimed, lame, blind—which, if you think about it, really is everyone born! And if they don't show up, we go out and urge them to come and join us (see Luke 14:7-14).

And the freedom the hymn invites us to at the end is interesting. We can't be free until the other guy is free. Sure, those of us who live in America might feel free. But we are in bondage we are not even aware of. We miss the joy. We miss out on the richness of a shared life with others who have been born. We get stuck in society's bog of anger and anxiety, isolation and trendiness.

The old saying is that you can never be happier than your unhappiest child. God wired the world so that we can never be free until others are free; we never grow until others can grow. God made us for connection, not to those like us but to those who are like God. And that is everyone born.

His Eye Is on the Sparrow

*A*nd every*thing* that is born. When I was a young pastor, I had a handful of members who were most unhappy with our "new hymnal" (which was nearly twenty years old at the time!) for several glaring omissions, the most egregious being "His Eye Is on the Sparrow."

"We should never have replaced the old *Cokesbury Hymnal!*" they said. Never mind the fact that they had plenty of old copies on hand and that none of my people even needed a book to sing "Why should I feel discouraged?" I just found it to be kind of corny, sentimental, and not made of strong enough stuff for the tough theology I was lifting up to my people. But despite my resistance, the hymn would not go away. A warbly soprano I loved dearly would regularly sing it as a solo.

I must have been just the kind of guy Jesus hoped would overhear when he told the people who didn't matter in the world's eyes that, in God's eyes, they were fabulously precious. Thankfully I've fallen back in love with this old hymn that I heard my grandmother sing while she went about her chores. Jesus asked us to see God's handiwork and sustenance in mere sparrows. Walter Brueggemann calls them "model citizens in the kingdom of God."[10] They nest inside the glorious Temple itself (see Psalm 84:3), too high to be shooed away by the priests and their acolytes. God feeds and clothes them, quite naturally. These non-acquisitive, trusting creatures have no worries. Easy for sparrows, I'd say.

The hymn asks, "Why should I be discouraged?" Let me count the ways. "Why should the shadows come?" is worth pausing over, not merely to count all the darkness that imposes itself in every life. Raymond Barfield, in his book on beauty and suffering, *Wager*, talks about learning to "reverence your shadow."[11] If you're in the world, you cast a shadow. It's proof you're here. If there's light, there is shadow, and if there's shadow, then there's light. Obviously—but that is why shadows come.

What's so lovely about the hymn is that it doesn't pledge or expect a quick fix or any fix at all. It's not that God will do what I ask or that God will repair everything tomorrow. It's simply that God cares. God sees. His eye is on the sparrow—as virtually worthless as a sparrow might seem to be. Jesus pointed out that five are sold for two pennies (see Luke 12:6)! God miraculously cares deeply for each one. God sees the sparrow, and God sees you and me. And it's not just a passing glance. Birdwatchers are patient, focused people, peering through their binoculars, noticing the slightest flutter of a feather, turn of the head, opening of the beak, or twitching of a talon.

Who was Jesus? Who is he? His nickname at birth was Emmanuel, "God with us." His parting words were "I will be with you." He is not a magical fulfiller of wishes or fixer of all troubles. He is with us. That's what my grandmother was singing about while sweeping and ironing. God's abiding presence infused her with joy and strength. She was dirt poor, and her arthritis pained her. But Jesus was her "portion," a lovely echo of Psalm 73:26.

Indeed, my grandmother and my warbly soprano friend soared to the climactic high note in the hymn, which occurs on "I'm free."

Not free American-style, the paltry notion that I can do whatever I dang well please. No, I'm free like a bird, as in Paul's ringing declaration, "For freedom Christ has set us free" (Gal. 5:1). Free from the cruel bondage of sin, anxiety, and fretting over self-worth or the terror of mortality.

Civilla Durfee Martin wrote the words to this hymn as a poem after visiting with her friend, Mrs. Doolittle, who had been bedridden for more than twenty years. Martin's husband asked Mrs. Doolittle her secret of joy in the thick of affliction. "His eye is on the sparrow, and I know he watches me." That was in 1905. It was back in maybe the year 28 that Jesus said pretty much the same thing. No wonder the hymn remains despite failing to make the cut with the hymnal committee. No wonder it's been recorded countless times. There are versions by Gladys Knight, Whitney Houston, Jennifer Holliday, Marvin Gaye, Sandi Patty, and (my personal favorite) Mahalia Jackson. Although I believe God always prefers it in the voice of my warbly soprano friend.

While I've Breath

Singers breathe. We all breathe of course, but singing requires a special kind of breathing. The song itself is breath morphed into notes and words. I wonder if Isaac Watts mused on this as he wrote "I'll Praise My Maker While I've Breath." He had read and contemplated Psalm 146 and wrote this hymn as a result.

The psalm is itself a wonder. The psalmist urges his own soul to praise the Lord "as long as I live." And why? Only God is trustworthy, not princes or other powers. Watts picks up on various themes in the psalm with lyrics like "Happy are those whose hopes rely on Israel's God, who made the sky and earth and seas, with all their train; whose truth forever stands secure." There is a social agenda to the psalm and to the hymn: This God saves the oppressed, feeds the poor, supports the fainting mind, and helps the stranger in distress.

You have breathed at least a dozen times, quite involuntarily, since you started reading this page. Breath is God's great gift of life. The moving air, the *ruach* (in Hebrew), the wind, the Spirit of God, is God giving life to you and all creation. The breath you just took while reading that sentence is a gift from God. Adam was some dirt into whom God breathed the breath of life. The first cry, the child's first communication to the world, says I am here! More important, it is a gasp for air. That first breath: the gift of life.

The apostle Paul pondered those days when we don't know how or what to pray. We simply sigh. That sigh of sorrow, of resignation, of despair is—speaking of miracles—God's Holy Spirit breathing and praying in us (see Romans 8:26). It may be that we praise God best when we are forlorn and do nothing but stammer, groan, and exhale.

If the breath you just took is a gift from God, then does it make sense to do whatever you wish? Isn't your life entirely owed to God?

I love the story that John Wesley, founder of Methodism and great reformer of the church, was lying on his deathbed in 1791, eighty-seven years old, having labored incessantly for God over a lifetime. Those who gathered nearby were stunned when, after many hours of silence, Wesley sang this hymn: "I'll praise my Maker while I have breath, and when my soul is lost in death, praise shall employ my nobler powers. My days of praise shall never be past, while life, and thought, and being last, or immortality endures."

While we have breath, we praise the Lord—in our minds, hearts, and lives. What will we do in heaven? Play golf? Eat delicious food? Maybe. But we will be in God's presence, which will elicit in us a stammering awe. Forever. We will do what we've not done nearly enough of here. We'll praise. We'll be amazed. We'll glorify. We'll love.

In the meantime we should engage in a life of praise. What does that look like? Father Gregory Boyle narrates how he responded to someone who asked, "In your work with previous gang members, when do you praise God?" He responded with the story of Mario, a much-tattooed ex-con, who became the tenderest, most merciful and compassionate of all Boyle's converts. He joined Boyle and spoke to a group of social workers—one of whom asked him what advice he would give to his children. He responded, "I just don't want my kids to turn out to be like me." She countered, "Why wouldn't you want your kids to turn out to be like you? You are gentle, you are kind, you are loving, you are wise . . . I *hope* your kids turn out to be like you." A huge ovation erupted from the crowd. Boyle believes this is the kind of praise God enjoys.[12]

Mystic Sweet Communion

*L*ent is a time of solitude and personal reflection, repentance and redemption. But it is not meant to be a season of loneliness. We do Lent with others, just as we always do Christianity with others. Thank God I don't believe simply by myself. I'm not saved for me, but to find myself in the body of Christ, the church universal. God has given us good company in this journey of faith. The old hymn, "Blest Be the Tie That Binds" reminds us that we "our mutual burdens bear." We bear one another's griefs and challenges. We're in this together.

But there is a line in that hymn that troubles me: "The fellowship of kindred minds." Nowadays churches and whole denominations split up because they think their minds aren't kindred anymore. Bitter disagreements pit us against one another. Some ferociously defend scripture and God's honor. Others just as ferociously want to welcome everyone and dream of progressing from rigidity to freedom and joy. We mirror the ugly partisanship of society. The devil laughs, high-fiving his minions.

In such a world, our most important hymn may be "The Church's One Foundation." That foundation is Jesus Christ. It is not my right thinking, and it is not thumping the other guys for thinking wrong. This great hymn envisions, as does scripture itself, Jesus embracing the church as "his holy bride." Those of us who are familiar with the church know this is aspirational. Perhaps we can realize that holiness if we take Jesus' hand. No one marries someone because they are perfect. We commit to the whole person, including flaws, missteps, and weaknesses.

Samuel Stone's eloquent words were set to music by Samuel Sebastian Wesley (whose songwriting genes were stellar, being Charles Wesley's grandson!). They echo not only dozens of scripture passages (see 1 Corinthians 3:11; John 3:5; Ephesians 5:26; Revelation 21:2; Philippians 2:10; Luke 12:37; Psalm 30:5; and Revelation 7:14 to name a few!) but also the great creeds of the church.

The Da Vinci Code and other popular books have tried to discredit creeds as manipulative manufactures foisted on church people. But our creeds are simply attempted digests of the long narrative of scripture. An ancient legend says that the apostles sat in a circle and composed a statement of faith: One said, "I believe in God the Father," and then another said, "and in Jesus Christ," and then another, "I believe in the Holy Spirit." That is a lovely thought. The assemblies of bishops who settled on the language of "God the Three-in-One" wrestled with all of scripture and decided that this was the best way to make sense of all we read about God. But it's not just some intellectual proposition demanding our assent. We have "union" and "mystic sweet communion" with this Three-in-One God. We are invited into that holy circle. That's what church is.

While extolling the grandeur of the church, our hymn acknowledges its foibles and challenges. We are "sore oppressed," yet truly more from within than from without. "By schisms rent asunder, by heresies distressed." When we bicker as Christians, when we pout and prefer our own way to the other guy's way, could it be that the saints in heaven, the famous ones like Francis of Assisi or Mother

Teresa, and the unfamous ones like my grandparents, actually cry out in agony over us?

"One Lord, one faith, one birth." Jesus, the church's one foundation, must weep every day that we are more than one faith and act like we are more than one birth. At the Last Supper, Jesus prayed, as he continues to pray right now, that we will be "one" (see John 17:21). The lovely truth is that we *are* one in Jesus' eyes. Can we learn to see ourselves as the one unified church that Jesus sees?

Lift High the Cross

$\mathscr{T}$o conclude this section of hymns that invite us to see as God sees and to see God, we hit refresh and recall that we see God most clearly in the cross of Christ. We erect a cross as the focal point of a sanctuary. People pray before a small cross. At my church, we conclude every sanctuary worship service by singing "Lift High the Cross" right after the benediction. This hymn is well over one hundred years old, but I didn't learn it until it appeared in our then-new United Methodist hymnal in 1989.

It is risky fixating on this idea of "Lift high the cross." During the Crusades, Christian warriors "took up the cross" by emblazoning a cross on their shields and armor and boasting that they were slaughtering Christ's foes in his name. The idea dates even further back, when Constantine defeated his foes to become emperor of Rome after he had some sort of vision or dream of a cross in the skies, which was then painted onto his soldiers' shields. He was barely a Christian, and any time armies crush and conquer, we have to wonder if they've understood Christ at all.

The image of lifting up the cross derives from John 12:32, where Jesus says, "When I am lifted up from the earth, I will draw all people to myself," and from John 3:14, where Jesus mystifies Nicodemus by alluding to Numbers 21:9, "And just as Moses lifted up the serpent in the wilderness, so must the Son of Man be lifted up."

It is baffling that Moses hoisted a bronze snake to heal the people. This notion of proudly lifting high the cross is stranger still. We've beautified and sentimentalized our crosses, but the cross on which Jesus was executed was cut from gnarled, twisted, ugly olive wood. Crucifixion wasn't something to brag about. The Romans nailed people up in public to intimidate and terrorize. The Bible itself said anyone killed hanging from a tree is cursed (see Deuteronomy 21:23). In the church's early decades, skeptics scoffed at a crucified Lord. Archaeologists have found some graffiti in Rome depicting a crucified donkey with the inscription "Alexamenos worships his god." Lift high the cross? Hide the thing. It is shameful, a bad joke. That's no way to grow a church.

But we are not ashamed. Step inside a church, and you'll see a cross. This is a place that doesn't avert its gaze from suffering. There is no denial of death here. Courage trumps security. "The love of Christ proclaim" is the secret shouted out loud when we lift the cross high. God isn't invisible, omnipotent, or ineffable. God came down to become one with us in our mortality. God showed us the divine heart and so much love.

Children are loved—but even the most intense parental love is exceeded and enveloped by God's love: "Each newborn servant of the Crucified bears on the brow the seal of him who died." Baptisms aren't cute. We seal this newest member of the body of Christ with the wonder of the cross. Is this cross offensive? Yes, but it is also alluring and magnetic, as mortals crave connection with God, especially in the hour of death. "Draw the world to thee." The cross can and does.

In the Middle Ages, a popular poem ("The Dream of the Rood") imagined what the cross thought leading up to and after the crucifixion:

> I was a sapling in the woods, then men cut me down and nailed the holy hero onto me, I felt him tremble, absorbed his sweat and blood, and after they took him down they threw me into a gully—but later they found me, lifted me high and adorned me with jewels and gold, and all look to me for healing and hope.

Traditionally, "Lift High the Cross" has been sung as a processional hymn at the beginning of worship, which makes so much sense. But I love it that we sing it as the recessional at our church. When we go out, it is then that we lift high the cross—in our lives, in our witness, in our daily existence. Lift the cross where the cross matters or not at all.

I remember being so moved when my theology professor in seminary spoke of Christians living a "cruciform" life. What is it for us to live in a way that conforms to, patterns itself on, and adores this cross of Christ? How do we lift high the love, the sacrifice, the forgiveness, and the total commitment?

For Christ's cross wasn't just "on a hill far away" once upon a time. It is now. As my pastor friend concludes all of her services: "The worship has ended; now the service begins."

With Joy Surround You

HYMNS OF BEAUTY

*D*oes it ever feel jarring or dissonant that Lent here in the northern hemisphere is a season of gray, ashes, darkness, and death, when outside everything is blooming, trees are greening, and nature is waking up after the long winter? God created beauty out there, partly just showing off, partly luring us into the beauty that is the heart and mind of God. From nature we learn how to be our natural, God-imaged selves. Trees, hummingbirds, and mountains glorify God simply by being themselves, and so we glorify God by connecting with them and growing into who we really are. God's final redemption isn't merely the saving of human souls but the redeemed grandeur of all creation.

Hearts Unfold like Flowers

$\mathcal{I}$t would be hard to imagine a day when the church didn't regularly enjoy the hymn "Joyful, Joyful, We Adore Thee." Our thanks belong to Henry Van Dyke, a traveler, professor of literature at Princeton, poet, and renowned preacher for putting poignant words to the "mighty chorus" of the finale of Ludwig van Beethoven's Ninth Symphony, which has rightly been called "one of the most precedent-shattering and influential compositions in the history of music."

> Its word-driven final movement is a declaration in favor of universal brotherhood, which explains why the Ninth is the work most often used to solemnize an important event—the opening of the United Nations, the signing of a peace treaty at the end of a war, the fall of the Berlin Wall . . . It is perceived as a vessel for a message that confers a quasi-religious yet nondenominational blessing on all "good" and "just" people, institutions, and enterprises.[1]

You don't need a complex understanding of the nature of Jesus Christ or a mass of scriptural knowledge to join enthusiastically in this hymn. God has splayed God's goodness and tender appeal to us all over creation for those who at least stop and look.

Van Dyke's most eloquent image might be "Hearts unfold like flowers before thee." Watch flowers. Don't just glance at them. Give it some time. Flowers take time. They don't sprout up in a jiffy. Gardeners understand that the cultivation and care of flowers requires patience, vigilance, and tenderness. The human heart yearns for a Lord and for faithful friends who are patient, vigilant, and tender. Flowers are fragile. That is their wonder. We know that a gust of wind, a scurrying squirrel, or a hard rain might damage them. They are transient like us, and yet they are lovely. Lent is about our transient mortality—which is our beauty too.

Flowers unfold. The bud gradually morphs, and then there's an opening up, a revelation of the beauty that has been hidden until that moment. Jesus preached on a hillside and pointed to the flowers all around and said, "This is God's tender care; this is God's nature; this is God strewing beauty all over the place—and this God will care for you" (see Matthew 6:28-30). He wasn't pointing to a finely manicured flower garden designed by a landscape architect. They were wildflowers popping up anywhere and everywhere. Like God's grace. They were unfolding like the hearts of the people of God.

Flowers don't seem to be trying hard. Effortlessly, they defy gravity and adorn even ugly, gray places. Their strength is under the ground, unseen, in the dark, where they reach down like the hungry soul for nourishment and ballast. Yet it's totally involuntary. Paul spoke of the "fruit of the Spirit," a poignant, truth-telling image. Fruit, like a flower, doesn't grit its teeth and strive valiantly to grow. Growth just happens to the fruit and to the flowers. The first fruit Paul names is *Love*, as it is the love of God that plants and nourishes flowers and our hearts. The second is *Joy*, which is what our hymn and Beethoven's stunning Ninth Symphony are all about—and what they create as we are dazzled and moved. Hearing about hearts unfolding opens up the heart to joy.

When we get to the second stanza, we find ourselves singing about the "flowery meadow." The heart that flowers is not alone. Rarely do you see just a single flower, unless it's been plucked by someone. Flowers grow together. Beethoven's Ninth was composed during tumultuous days in the nineteenth century when nations couldn't get along and people within nations loathed one another almost more than they loathed the other nations. This symphony has been called "a one-of-a-kind counterargument to the retrograde tendencies of the day."[2] Into such a culture of rancor, distrust, and division, Beethoven picked an old poem and set it to music that undeniably draws everyone in. The repeated refrain is "Alle Menschen werden Brüder": All men become brothers. All people become siblings. We really are family.

English speaking choirs sing these words in German, giving the *w* in werden a *v* sound, and trying their darnedest to do something resembling a Germanic sound with that daunting *u* umlaut, that ü. The noble, bumbling effort to speak in someone else's mother tongue, longing to be understood, hoping to be spoken to in reply: This is love, this is joy, this is hope. Beethoven's declared goal when scribbling down all those notes and words was "to liberate mankind through art."[3] Perhaps that was God's intention when in creation God thought *I'll throw in some flowers for good measure, to liberate my people, so their hearts will open up to me and to one another*.

Morning by Morning, New Mercies

*H*ow odd that a hymn would be based on a text from the Old Testament book of Lamentations: "The steadfast love of the Lord never ceases, his mercies never come to an end; they are new every morning; great is your faithfulness" (3:22-23). Lamentations is a searing, sorrowful, Lent-like lament over the destruction of the holy city of Jerusalem, including Mount Zion, God's holy Temple, the center of the known world to the Israelites. To such forlorn, crushed people, teetering on the brink of despair, a word emerged about God's love unceasing, about mercy each morning.

Israelites would have heard the idea of "morning mercy" as an echo of what their ancestors had experienced in the wilderness. Having been miraculously delivered from harsh bondage under the cruel Pharaoh, Israelites found themselves in a desert where there was no food (see Exodus 16). Out in the wilderness with no food supply, they could only poke their heads out every morning and look again each day for God's sustenance lying on the ground. *Manna.* It was nothing fabulous. It was just enough. Was it tasty? It was sufficient. Ever since, manna has stood as the perfect symbol of God's daily mercy, sufficient for the day and to be sought the next day just as hungrily.

There really is something about a morning, even if you aren't as exuberant as Curly in the musical *Oklahoma*: "Oh what a beautiful mornin', oh what a beautiful day, I've got a wonderful feelin' everything's goin' my way." Even the dourest among us might feel a bit like Quentin, the lawyer in Arthur Miller's *After the Fall*, who battled much anxiety but optimistically declared, "With all this darkness, the truth is that every morning when I awake, I'm full of hope . . . I'm like a boy! For an instant, there's some—unformed promise in the air."[4]

It's as if God created the world—morning and evening, sun rising, setting, darkness, and then the dawn—in imitation of Easter, which did dawn on people in the morning. Each morning is a little Easter, a new beginning even for the most encrusted, stuck, pessimistic among us. The sun has risen. Again. What to do with another day? It's just a day. And yet my lifetime is nothing but a day, another day, a whole bunch of days.

The Israelites were stuck in the wilderness, not for forty minutes or forty days but forty years. Most didn't live to see the fruition of their dreams. They died out there with their visions unrealized. Isn't that life in this world? How tragic and yet marvelous it is that Moses—yes, Moses, the man of God, the one God spoke to face to face—died out there with all the others. No matter how many days you get, like Moses you never reach total fulfillment.

The hymn clarifies: "Thy compassions, they fail not." The hymn and the Bible never even hint that God fixes everything or that God makes it all chipper and comfy. But God's compassion "fails not." Isn't that what we need at the end of the day—or at the beginning of the day? If you've been with someone who's dying, it's not about a panicked attempt to rescue them. It's letting go, sending the beloved into God's eternal compassions. There are no worries, even for the dying, because God has granted "pardon for sin and a peace that endureth . . . Strength for today and bright hope for tomorrow."

This can be trusted because "Great is thy faithfulness." Ancient people trembled before their moody and capricious deities. Modern people tremble when they ponder that it's all chance, or that "everything happens for a reason," or that "it's all up to me." Israel and today's Christians know and can trust—every morning and all day—in the greatness and endless bounty of God's faithfulness.

Purple Mountain Majesties

$\mathcal{I}$t seems to be part of God's strange dispensation that Christians wind up divided on a great many things, driving one another crazy and yet stuck with one another, perhaps to stretch, grow, and certainly learn some mercy. Our so-called "patriotic" hymns are a fair example. Some people avoid singing them at all costs, fearing we might confuse patriotism or nationalism with the gospel—which isn't American but international and even cosmic in scope. Others adore singing them because they touch something deep inside, a treasuring of nation, home, sacrifices for freedom, and a profound pride in who we are.

"America the Beautiful" manages to straddle these two divided groups. The beauty of creation is lauded in a poetic vision of "spacious skies," "amber waves of grain," and "purple mountain majesties." The prayer, "God shed his grace on thee," is one we surely need to pray in every generation. The humility in "God mend thine every flaw" in stanza three is unarguable. We might debate what's a flaw and what isn't, but we all know we need to confess and seek the divine miracle of mending those flaws that we can't mend ourselves. Let us pray this always.

The middle stanza can be construed as militaristic, rah-rah patriotism, but it need not be so. All countries have their heroes, their young who have died in combat. All nations grieve them, memorialize them, and even commend them to God. Let's ponder this: All nations, oddly, are like us. Americans love to feel that they are special. They *are* special, but so are Italians, Koreans, and Kenyans. God seems to have made all of us so that we take deep pride in our homeland. *Fealty* is a lovely word that captures the sense of loyalty, allegiance, and attachment that people feel about their own place.

I've gotten to know Haitians and Liberians and have preached the gospel in both places. Americans, in their ignorance, mistakenly pity nations where there has been civil conflict and a relative lack of economic success. They neglect to see the resilience, creativity, and faithfulness to God in the land and the people. Haitians and Liberians are immensely proud of their country. They admire the beauty, the tenderness of their people, and the resilient hope they have for the day when God will mend their flaws and shed God's grace on them. They have their purple mountains and amber waves too.

Katharine Lee Bates was a professor at Wellesley. In 1893, she made a cross-country trek in a covered wagon all the way to Pike's Peak, and then she wrote this hymn. For her, America wasn't an image, a waved flag, or a fist raised in political rancor. It was an expansive place she had experienced. Ponder the diverse locations, landscapes, weather, people, and buildings ("alabaster cities"!) she observed on her long journey. It is quite simply "majesty."

For those who fret that national hymns divert us from the kind of social justice action God requires of all people everywhere, it's worth noting that Bates was herself a social activist. She worked tirelessly for justice for Hispanics (and this was during the Spanish-American War when Hispanics were sorely hated and mistreated), women's suffrage, world peace, and fairness and welcome for immigrants and all people of color. She enjoyed a decades-long relationship with Katharine Cowan, which in those days was dubbed a "Boston marriage."

America the beautiful indeed. Americans can love America, and if we slow down and notice, there is a subtle wonder, a diverse fabric of place, geography, growing things, color, and people. That's America. Bates quite clearly was passionate about America and held the highest possible, godly vision of the place. Remember: God told us, through his prophet, "Seek the welfare of the city where I have sent you" (Jer. 29:7). Seek the welfare of the alabaster cities, the small towns, the crossroads, the villages, and even the mountains and flatlands. They all belong to God. They are all our field of mission. America the beautiful. Just like all the other nations.

The Song of Harvest Home

*T*he sun rises and sets. Spring dawns, and then fall descends. This is the grace of the seasons, the fruits of time, the pace of life. Who are the thankful people we ask to come when we sing "Come, Ye Thankful People, Come"? We don't mean the well-mannered who habitually write thank-you notes. And we don't mean those who have so many comforts that they bask in ease and feel quite blessed by God.

A deep disposition of humility doesn't ask for all that much and is pleasantly surprised by what little might come. It is not taking credit but always feeling like a lucky dog. Gratitude isn't natural or spontaneous. Infants and toddlers don't rise up and thank their parents for their nourishment and embraces. Parents struggle to teach their children to say thank you. We too need considerable tutoring and practice to be "thankful people."

Come ye who read this book: Know that we labor at a terrible disadvantage with respect to our ancestors and to people around the globe. We have much, and our society's ideology teaches us that we have earned it, deserve it, and really should have more. We are consumers after all, and consumers aren't allowed to feel contentment, which is the fruit of gratitude.

Perhaps it's aspirational when the hymn calls us "thankful people." We dream of being deeply thankful. The hymn was written for people closer to the earth, tangibly connected to simple products like food. "Raise the song of harvest home; all is safely gathered in, ere the winter storms begin." People in biblical times even had a spring harvest during the season we know as Lent.

Now we are insulated from the production of our own food, and so we forget how precarious it all is. Will it rain? What if the winds are fierce? What if my back goes out and I can't plow? Yet we can learn to ponder our food. God made a world where the ground is fertile. Someone plowed, planted, and harvested. Someone processed and packed the food. Someone drove it to the store. Someone shelved it. Someone's working the checkout. Someone cooks and hands me a plate. Wow. There are so many people to thank or be thankful for!

Gratitude seems to dawn on us quite naturally when something extraordinary happens: A surprise bouquet of flowers arrives, mom survives her surgery, your son visits unexpectedly. But Rabbi David Wolpe reminds us, "There is no trick to being grateful for that which is rare and special. To be grateful for that which is always there is difficult."[5] Gratitude looks around and notices what is ever-present: the grass, a constant friend, breathing, gravity, the roof over your head, eyesight, bread, water, or a spouse who stays. Gratitude looks around and looks back, not in regret or grief but seeing what has been a blessing.

And then gratitude looks forward. How lovely is this hymn's reflection on the astonishing blessing of the harvest before winter, perceiving in it a foretaste of God's gathering us home. "For the Lord our God shall come, and shall take the harvest home." Just as the farmer winnows what is plucked, leaving the chaff and preserving the wheat, so God shall "in that day all offenses purge away."

Jesus' story about the wheat and tares is a parable about how to be the church: We're better together, and when we try to be a wheat church that purges the tare interlopers, we become smug, unthankful harmers of others, ourselves, and God. But it's also a parable about our souls. There's some good wheat in there, but gosh, there are so many weeds.

But that won't be true forever. "Even so, Lord, quickly come, bring thy final harvest home; gather thou thy people in, free from sorrow, free from sin." Many Christians through history have longed for Christ to come and finish things, to bring us home. In antebellum America, the enslaved people sang "Soon I will be done with the troubles of the world." But many others—possibly us—are so attached to the things of this world that they would prefer Christ stay away for quite some time. Even so, Lord quickly come.

Martin Rinkart composed "Now Thank We All Our God" during the Thirty Years' War and the pestilence of 1637, when he was conducting up to fifty funerals a day, including his wife's. What strong stuff, what gentle fibers are such people made of, who know how to give thanks in the thick of a crushing intensity of suffering. It's a humble surprisedness at whatever good happens and an unshakable confidence that God will come and bring that final harvest home.

Music for Thy Lord to Hear

$\mathscr{T}$hrough various twists, turns, and translations, we have in our English hymnals a song St. Francis of Assisi composed and sang in Italian in the thirteenth century: "All Creatures of Our God and King." How alluring and countercultural is his hymn to creation! Most modern people think that nature is for our use, to photograph for Facebook, or to protect out of fear of climate disaster. Francis believed that even the smallest, most unappealing thing in nature praises God just by being. Testaments to God's beauty, power, and grace are all over the place.

The hymn invites us—not just while singing but all the time— to develop eyes and ears to perceive beauty where many miss it. "O sister water, flowing clear, make music for thy Lord to hear." We focus too much on whether we like our religious music or not. It's for God to hear. All our senses were made by God so we would notice God and the things of God, including barnacles, tumbleweed, a scurrying cockroach, and the unwittingly funny clownfish. And we should notice out loud so God will hear.

"Ye lights of evening, find a voice!" Earlier in this book we noted that Aristotle believed stars left a trail of music as they travelled through the heavens.[6] Science says that they do not, but that misses the point Aristotle was making about harmony and beauty in the skies. He couldn't hear the music he thought the stars were making, just as we can't hear the music we are sure they don't. Still, what we see up there is a kind of evangelism, isn't it? "The heavens are telling the glory of God" (Ps. 19:1). Look at the world. Notice. Add music. Our hymns simply harmonize with the lights of the evening.

This is true no matter your mood. When Francis wrote this song, he had tuberculosis, was nearly blind, was in constant pain, and was emaciated by sporadic bleeding from gaping wounds in his hands, feet, and side. His friars were bickering. And he was emotionally drained.

And yet, instead of sinking into despondency or pleading with God to fix everything, Francis began to hum. His aching hands took up a pen and began to write history's most soaring paean of praise to God. What is the antidote to despair? For Francis, it was praise.

Astronomers, geologists, and biologists can show us the science in numbers and facts. For Francis, the sun was his brother and the moon his sister. Children might intuit these things, if their devotion to the little book *Goodnight, Moon* is any indication. We aren't remote observers, but siblings. And God is our Parent. This personal kinship is what we've lost over centuries of building, paving over paradise, and stringing up things electric. Having forgotten how to honor God in all that God has made us, leaves us, others, and the world dishonored.

Francis had cultivated his attentiveness and devotion to beauty long before those painful years at the end of his life. Becoming a noticer, one who glorifies God by letting your jaw drop in awe over the slightest wonder, is the curriculum of a lifetime, a retraining of the senses to discern personal, family connections. Francis didn't speak *about* flowers; he spoke *to* the flowers—as does his hymn, inviting them to join with us in song. Francis encouraged the flowers to praise the Lord. He would pause along the road and address plants, a meadow, a brook, and even the wind.

The animal kingdom was extended family to Francis. Science has in recent decades been trying to teach this to religious people, who nonsensically resist the lovely truth of our kinship, our physiological interconnection with all God's creatures. Chimpanzees are our close cousins genetically? We're all descended from some common primate? Francis would slap his knee and say, "I knew it!"

Stone bird feeders memorialize Francis's devotion to birds. But he went beyond feeding birds and actually preached to them, exhorting them to praise and love the Lord in gratitude for wings, feathers, air to fly in, trees to nest in, and food to eat.[7] His friends followed suit. St. Anthony, not to be outdone by Francis's birds sermon, preached to fish, reminding them to be grateful for fins to swim and gills to breathe underwater, how they were saved during Noah's flood, how one of their own saved Jonah, and how another gave a coin to Jesus himself.[8]

This family feel resonates through every stanza of Francis's hymn: "O brother wind, air, clouds and rain . . . O brother fire who lights the night, providing warmth, enhancing sight." For Francis, that unbreakable kinship you have with family—the people you're stuck with—informs the fifth and sixth stanzas of our hymn, as we will see in our next section.

Of Tender Heart,
Forgiving Others

$\mathcal{A}$fter four stanzas of imaginative, kaleidoscopic, eloquent interaction with all of creation, stanza five of "All Creatures of Our God and King" pulls us back into the inter-human realm with an unexpected jolt: "All ye who are of tender heart, forgiving others, take your part." One moment we're in a happy conversation with birds, wind, stars, and the running brook. The next moment we're talking about forgiving people.

Here's the backstory. After Francis composed his canticle, he and his friends prayed and sang it while loitering about the streets or heading to the market or doing their chores. Assuming he had finished writing the song, Francis's friends were puzzled when he added a verse—with strict instructions to his friars to sing the expanded version in the city square on a certain day, knowing the bishop and the mayor would be there. The ears of the most powerful men in the city perked up when they heard it; they knew it had been written for them. They had fallen into intense conflict with one another, spewing angry words and flinging accusations.

What had Francis added for their benefit?

"Be praised, my Lord, for those who pardon through Your love and bear witness and trial.

"Blessed are those who endure in peace
for they will be crowned by You, Most High."

After the friars finished their song, these two authorities met in the middle, and with "great kindness and love they embraced and kissed each other."[9]

How do you heal a quarrel between stubborn people? Francis could have taken sides or fumed at them. Instead, he sang the often-forgotten truth that reconciliation is God's work and will. The antidote to despair is praise. The antidote to human turmoil might just be praise too.

Just as God made sun, moon, stars, birds, and fish, God made us. We're made to praise God and all other creatures. This includes the one who's tough to love and the one who's hurt you. Forgiveness is the route back to the creation God intended. Forgiveness is seeing the other person as created and preserved by God, intended for praise and glory. Reconciliation happens; it must happen. It's the restoration of God's good order. It's finding our way back to truth.

Our hymn invites "All ye who are of tender heart, forgiving others." Is forgiveness something you do if you feel forgiving toward another? Or is it at the core of Christian being? I think of those amazing Amish people who forgave the family of Charles Roberts for his shooting spree in 2006 that killed five Amish children. I think of Corrie Ten Boom, who looked on as a Nazi soldier killed her sister Betsie. Encountering him years later, she found a way to forgive him.

After Charles Roberts fired on children, the Amish didn't huddle and ask what forgiveness is. They had been schooled over a long time, as had Corrie Ten Boom. They were prepared deep in their bones to act as they did. So we practice forgiveness in small things around the house, at work, and in the neighborhood.

It's all about power. Forgiveness is the relinquishment of power. The power of blame. The power of fault-finding. The power of feeling "right." When the strong befriend the weak, dignity and strength are imparted to the weak—although in reality, dignity and strength flow both ways.

Here are a couple of images that might help. Donald Gowan points out that "As mothers and fathers hurt by their wayward children, husbands hurt by their unfaithful wives, and brothers who have been betrayed, find something in themselves to make it possible to work toward a restored relationship, that something, multiplied many times, is present, and in fact originates in God."[10] It's riveting that the Hebrew word for *mercy* is the same as the word for *womb*. How do we have mercy on those who came out of the womb? How do we labor literally toward a womb-like relationship with the vulnerable?

How transformative is it that the Greek word rendered *forgive* in the New Testament, *aphiēmi*, means simply "to let go." When we hold a grievance close, we're the ones getting devoured. The day comes when we let go. We needn't have warm fuzzy feelings toward the one who damaged us, but we can let go of the enmity, the grip of rage, and the recollection of being wronged. Jesus did this with and for us. He let it all go on the cross. He forgave and forgives. What is it we pray constantly? "Forgive us our trespasses, as we forgive those who trespass against us." O ye of tender heart.

Our Sister, Bodily Death

$\mathcal{F}$rancis still wasn't done. Edition three of his song added a stanza praising the truest of all true realities: "Our sister, bodily death." Suffering intensely, Francis welcomed his own death, as have so many martyrs and great saints who knew they were about to be welcomed into God's eternal presence. His words were:

Be praised, My Lord, for our sister, bodily death.
Whom no one living can escape.
Woe to those who die in sin.
Blessed are those who discover Thy holy will.
The second death will do them no harm.[11]

How fitting an end to his song praising nature. For something "natural" is coming our way, and the question is whether we will be ready to welcome this unwanted, yet natural stranger. We have all known and loved people who have been sick and tired for so long that they were just done and ready to go. My mother was like that. But Francis was only forty-four. We marvel at the way Francis died in such unified oneness with nature. Made of dust, we return to dust. We are of the earth, one with nature. Lent is the peaceful realization of our mortality.

During the darkest days of his life, Henri Nouwen wrote,

You are so afraid of dying alone . . . Maybe the death at the end of your life won't be so fearful if you can die well now. Yes, the real death—the passage from time into eternity, from the transient beauty of this world to the lasting beauty of the next, from darkness into light—has to be made now.[12]

Can Francis's canticle and our hymn ease us into a safe place to begin to befriend death to self, illusion, and phony fantasies? Can we begin to discover the new life after death that God fashions in this life before our final death?

Death, the great terror, is the ever-present reality dogging all of us. Ernest Becker won the Pulitzer Prize for his brilliant psychological analysis of the way *The Denial of Death* (his book's title) frames all of our anxiety, our drivenness, our breakdowns.[13] The Christian message isn't that we needn't fret about death. Paul suggested that we grieve heavily—but we do so as those who have hope (see 1 Thessalonians 4:13-18). Death can be embraced, even as we tenaciously hold on to the wonder that is this life.

Jesus showed us the way by crying out in desperate rage, "My God, why have you forsaken me?" He showed us how to love this life so much we don't want to let it go. And yet Francis, having suffered for several years from poor health, knew his time was short, and so he sang of that one inevitable moment that all created things come to: "Our sister, bodily death."

There can be something gentle, even beautiful about many deaths, though not all. Francis's was relatively peaceful. He asked to be carried to the little stone church, the Porziuncula, he had rebuilt with his own hands. He had started a hospital on the premises for people with leprosy, whom he welcomed just as Abraham welcomed strangers by the Oaks of Mamre (see Genesis 18). And he welcomed death just as Abraham was believed to have welcomed Death itself when it came knocking at his door. (The story is in *The Testament of Abraham,* an apocryphal book from the first century CE).

At the end, Francis said to his closest friends, "I have done what is mine to do. Now it is for you to do what is yours to do." And he was gathered up with the angels into the heart of God.

As a pastor, I've stood in hospital rooms with families of the dying who sing hymns together—often the hymns portrayed in this book. It's moving. What better way to lift up the beloved and usher them toward heaven than on the praises of God's historic church through the ages? And then, if the book of Revelation is a reliable clue, death isn't the end of our singing, but a door through which we enter heaven's magnificent choir, where "mortals join the mighty chorus" of saints and angels who occupy their time singing praises to God. Our days of praise shall never be past because of what we've been journeying toward through Lent: what Jesus accomplished for himself, God, and all of creation during Holy Week.

Stony the Road

HYMNS OF HOLY WEEK

*F*inally, we reach the climax of the year, truly the center of human history, the axis on which everything turns: Holy Week. Day by day, we ponder what Jesus did—his courage, his commitment, his immense compassion—and how the events of a single week from so long ago still resonate with us today.

The Stories of Jesus

$\mathcal{O}$ur uncertainty about what to do with Palm Sunday mirrors the confusion of the eyewitnesses when Jesus rode that donkey into Jerusalem. We make it cute and cheerful, with children waving palm leaves as we sing chipper melodies like "Tell Me the Stories of Jesus." The crowd back then was seized with joy and excitement, apparently not understanding who Jesus was, all he was about, why he was coming to Jerusalem in this way, or the ominous fate that awaited him. The rock opera *Jesus Christ Superstar* captures this paradox: The frenzied crowd sings "Hey J. C., J. C., won't you smile at me?" and then "Won't you fight for me?" and then "Won't you die for me?" while Caiaphas begins his plot to silence them and J. C.

We earnestly ask, "Tell me the stories of Jesus"—the stories that Jesus told and the stories that were told about him. He was a spellbinding storyteller. But the stories of Jesus are so much more than mere entertainment. Clarence Jordan compared Jesus' parables to the Trojan horse. It looks good. You let it in and then—Bam!

Why was anyone shocked when Jesus stormed back into Jerusalem the day after Palm Sunday and upset the order in the Temple? The stories Jesus told should have prepared everyone for this; upsetting order is exactly what they do. A Samaritan is the hero and the holy people are hard-hearted. A farmer is eager to waste seed. A party is thrown for a ne'er-do-well son who'd squandered his father's hard-earned living. Day laborers who worked one hour are paid the same as those who toiled all day. He blessed the meek and narrated how to love enemies. He disrespected Caesar, Herod, and the high priests.

Tell me the stories *about* Jesus. In a contest with the devil, he didn't assume power. He touched the untouchables and hung out with the unclean and despised, including nasty tax collectors and tawdry prostitutes. He defended his friends when they had blatantly violated the sabbath. He spoke words of woe on the nice, pious people. His table manners were atrocious: he upbraided his hosts for inviting the wrong people, and he let a woman of questionable reputation give his feet an oil massage. He claimed that he was literally God come down to earth. What could be more laughable, offensive, and downright dangerous? He even disrespected his own mother.

"Tell me the stories of Jesus I love to hear." I do love them, but they make my head spin, and I begin to understand why the authorities were lying in wait for him, why their dragnet was beginning to close, and why they could not let him continue. The Pharisees, with unwitting irony, huddled up and declared, "If we let him go on thus, everyone will believe in him." Caiaphas chimed in, "It is expedient for you that one man should die for the people, and that the whole nation should not perish" (John 11:48-50, rsv).

Knowing that bloodthirsty men were waiting to attack him in the city, Jesus left the relative safety of the Mount of Olives, descending right past a garden called Gethsemane where he would return to pray (and get himself arrested) just four nights later. He passed through the Kidron valley and then up the hill into the teeth of violent men who hated him. What courage he had.

This seems like a moment that children should be shielded from. And yet, maybe the children were the ones who got it, or at least knew that he was the One. He had always welcomed them, in an era when children were supposed to stay quiet and out of sight. He had always said you have to become like them if you're going to be deployed in God's kingdom. So "into the city I'd follow the children's band." We follow their lead, always. At my church, the kids love handing out the palm leaves. They wave them with joy and gusto, while the grown-ups clutch theirs and wave them tentatively, if at all.

What does *Hosanna* mean? We think of it as a churchy way of saying "Yay!" But the Hebrew is more desperate; it means "Save us!" or "Lord, help!" It is fascinating that a single word can imply both a dark cry for a miracle and also an expression of joy. Is it in anticipation of the joy that will come when the help has arrived? Is it a dream, even a lovely declaration of certain hope? The one who elicited those shouts—then and now—has a similar name. Jesus, *yeshu'a*, means "Lord, help!" God in Jesus became one with the cry of humanity through the ages for divine aid. He is that cry, and he is the answer to that cry. So, from the depths of our being, having heard the stories of Jesus, we cry, "Hosanna! Jesus! Hosanna!" He answered on Good Friday.

Save Us from Weak Resignation

A fair criticism of most Christian hymnals is that the overall feel is of a spirituality that is disconnected from or uninterested in the social troubles of the world. Hymns speak to the interior life, personal struggles, sin, and doubt, but very rarely do they speak to God's call for us to be the light to the nations, the salt of the earth, and instigators of change. Perhaps hymnals have forgotten about Holy Monday.

We do see hints here and there of social engagement. Frank Mason North's hymn from 1905, "Where Cross the Crowded Ways of Life," speaks to "the cries of race and clan, above the noise of selfish strife, we hear your voice, O Son of man." There had to be a racket echoing all over the Temple precincts as Jesus overturned tables, scattered coins across the floor, and sent turtledoves squawking as they flew away. Shocked money changers shouted in resistance, and Jesus tried to explain himself while enraged.

Harry Emerson Fosdick's "God of Grace and God of Glory" prays a much-needed but rarely found prayer in hymns: "Grant us courage." We need it because "Lo! the hosts of evil round us scorn thy Christ, assail his ways. . . . Cure thy children's warring madness, bend our pride to thy control. . . . Save us from weak resignation." Have we sung these words in light of our political and social challenges?

Some Methodists might be surprised to find the so-called "Black National Anthem" in their hymnals: "Lift Every Voice and Sing," which resounds with "the harmonies of liberty." Jesus wasn't campaigning for Civil Rights *per se* when he cleansed the Temple on Holy Monday. But he was acting with immense courage and strength. He refused to tolerate what was not of God. He "got in the way" (as John Lewis said). He used his body not just to talk but to enact that revolution.[1]

Jesus acted. He stepped boldly into the long tradition of prophetic action in God's name—from Moses striding into the courts of Pharaoh to Ezekiel's symbolic cutting of his hair and beard. That tradition has gone on. The labor for God's goodness in the real world is long and painful, requiring resilience and uncompromising hope, as that "national anthem," composed by brothers James Weldon Johnson and John Rosamond Johnson, reminds us. "Stony the road we trod, bitter the chastening rod." During Holy Week, Jesus' feet felt stones in the road, and his back felt the brutal lashing of the rod. "Yet with a steady beat, have not our weary feet come to the place for which our fathers sighed." During the Montgomery bus boycott, an elderly woman nicknamed "Mother Pollard" politely refused many efforts to give her rides. Her regular reply became a motto in the movement: "My feets is tired, but my soul is rested."[2] Indeed. "Let us march on till victory is won."

Hymns can help us live into the already/not yet truths of Christian existence. We sing "Victory in Jesus," but that victory is not yet fully won. Jesus died to redeem the world, but clearly it is far from redeemed. Jesus cleansed the Temple, but corruption has riddled all the institutions that claim to exist for Jesus. The wins of today witness to the larger win that is now inevitable but not yet fully evident. I love J. Christiaan Beker's summary of what the apostle Paul dreamed for the church to be on this side of eternity: "the avant-garde of the new creation in a hostile world, creating beachheads in this world of God's dawning new world and yearning for the day of God's visible lordship over his creation."[3]

Jesus and his people wade ashore and establish a toehold like those courageous soldiers on D-Day: The triumph was assured, but so much work remained. The road ahead will be stony and long, requiring the kind of sacrifice Jesus offered, not just for us but to inspire us. We are not alone. We walk the path blazed by Jesus, the prophets, and a host of heroes, some famous, others unremembered by history. "We have come over a way that with tears has been watered." But the very tangibility of acting for God's kingdom is beautiful and invigorating.

When John Lewis was shown a photo taken of himself as a teenager leaving jail after having been beaten and arrested for peaceful demonstration, he studied it for a moment and said, "I had never had that much dignity before. It was exhilarating—it was something I had earned, the sense of the independence that comes to a free person."[4] Jesus was the free one, setting us free, granting us dignity. When we find ourselves "treading our path through the blood of the slaughtered," we are one with Jesus and anticipate his victory.

Wonderful Words

$\mathcal{I}$n 1874, a "singing evangelist" named Philip Bliss wrote a sunny, chipper hymn, "Wonderful Words of Life," and set it to a cheerful tune with kids in mind:

> These simple words and music were written to be sung by children. The purpose of this song is to promote in the child a love and appreciation of the scriptures. It speaks to and for the child in all of us.[5]

Yet the child in all of us has ready access to the actual words of Jesus. It's one thing to sing about them; it's another to hear them, grapple with them, absorb them, and then live into them. Jesus' words usually are shockers, words that excavate the soul, diagnose unseen maladies, name what ails us, and catapult us out of our comfort zones into radical action for Jesus. When Mark Helprin spoke of books that are "hard to read, that could devastate and remake one's soul, and that, when they were finished, had a kick like a mule,"[6] he could have been describing Jesus' "wonderful words of life."

"Sing them over again to me." Jesus spoke sternly to the devil. Jesus spoke tenderly to those others despised, and then he uttered words of woe to the pious who weaponized the scriptures and judged others. Jesus blessed the meek, declared anger and lust to be against the law, and dared us to love our enemies. Jesus' wonderful words of life were spoken to people he wasn't supposed to speak to at all: Samaritans, tax collectors, prostitutes, and people with leprosy. His dinner conversations were impolite toward hosts he might have thanked. He forgave his executioners without them even asking.

We dare not forget that so many of Jesus' "wonderful words" were uttered in the very Temple precincts where, the day before, he had alarmed and appalled the authorities by driving out the money changers. What courage. Instead of lying low for a while, Jesus walked into the teeth of peril, as if to make sure we'd listen. Jesus had a lot to say, more than two hundred verses even though he knew that those who were plotting to kill him were prowling in the crowds (see Matthew 21:23–25:46).

The Pharisees didn't hear Jesus' words as "wonderful words," and so they strategized "to entangle him in his talk," asking if it was lawful to pay taxes to Caesar; his ingenious reply left them stammering. Jesus' words to God in Gethsemane were sheer agony, and on the cross he screamed his despairing God-forsakenness. "Sing them over again to me, wonderful words of life." Then after Easter he spoke words of calming peace and asked Peter if he loved him in return.

Jesus' stories and teaching turned the known world on its ear. Callicles's complaint to Socrates describes equally well the power of Jesus' words:

> If you are serious and what you say is true, then surely the life of us mortals must be turned upside down and apparently we are everywhere doing the opposite of what we should.[7]

Do not lay up treasure on earth. The last will be first. He who would save his life will lose it. Not my will but your will be done. Sell all you have and give it to the poor. I have come to set father against son.

Our hymn says, "Let me more of their beauty see . . . words of life and beauty." Instead of shivering or devising ways to dodge or explain away his words, perhaps we should ask to see their true beauty. For they are beautiful because they are the words of the only truly beautiful One. We try to do beautiful things for this beautiful One, and we become surprisingly but truly beautiful ourselves as we do.

Rabbi Jonathan Sacks notices how Moses insisted that the Israelites teach their children about the exodus from Egypt: "About to gain their freedom, the Israelites were told that they had to become a nation of educators." Indeed, for Christianity and Judaism "freedom is won, not on the battlefield, not in the political arena, nor in the courts . . . but in the human imagination and will. To defend a country, you need an army. But to defend a free society you need schools."[8]

Jesus' wonderful words take us free people to school. We absorb Jesus' beautiful thoughts. And then we "sweetly echo the gospel call." The child learns to talk by soaking in the parents' talk. And the child then speaks inevitably as the parents have spoken, with their accents and emphases, their phrasing and expressions. Our words are to echo Jesus' wonderful words. This doesn't mean sugary sweet piety; Jesus never talked that way. Instead we forgive, speak with the lonely, tell the truth, cry out in agony, and, above all, name mercy and hope as our beloved realities. Such words are "all so freely given, wooing us to heaven."

Abide with Me

*S*ome hymns are associated in our minds by habit or by common use with particular situations. "Abide with Me" gets sung at funerals.

Henry Francis Lyte wrote the words when his health was deteriorating rapidly back in 1847. He probably wrote it, or most of it, on the day he surrendered his pastoral work in England to travel to Italy to recuperate. He died along the way in France. Sorrow, love, and a glimmer of hope glow from the embers of this hymn.

Yet it can and should be a hymn for the living. Lyte probably was thinking of that moment when the risen Jesus had caught up with the two forlorn disciples on the road to Emmaus. When they came to their village, they said, "Abide with us; for it is toward evening, and the day is far spent" (Luke 24:29, KJV). In that moment, it wasn't a lonely soul asking Jesus to stay. It was a fellowship of three.

The Bible doesn't say much if anything about the Holy Trinity. But we know God is eternally a fellowship of three, abiding, staying, loving, and sharing. I love the Rublev icon *The Trinity,* which depicts Father, Son, and Holy Spirit sitting around a table together. That's God, this fellowship of three. Just as the Emmaus story invites you the reader to join the threesome of Jesus and the other two, God's holy club invites you to pull up a chair on that open fourth side of the table.

The image of Jesus staying, lingering, and abiding is a constant in John's Gospel. Jesus saw two of John's disciples and stayed with them just before he saw Nathanael standing under a fig tree (see John 1:35-48). Jesus lingered mid-day with the Samaritan woman at the well (see John 4). During Holy Week, as in all his visits to Jerusalem, he stayed at the home of Mary, Martha, and Lazarus (see John 12:1-8). We don't know what Jesus did all day on Holy Wednesday. He probably just abided at home with his three friends. Then, at his last supper, Jesus invited his friends to "abide in me as I abide in you" (John 15:4). They overheard his prayer, including that he abides in the Father and the Father abides in him (see John 17:21). He was nearing his end. But the abiding is for them, for the rest of their lives, for the life of the church.

Every day, dusk and darkness remind us that our mortal lives are brief. "Fast falls the eventide; the darkness deepens." Indeed, "other helpers fail." So faith is turning to God, "help of the helpless." Loss and death are not merely our own, but the death of others we've loved, others we've never known, and nameless victims of evil, not to mention the death of dreams and illusions. Heartbreak, aging, and even graduation and retirement—transitions we celebrate—are losses. In the thick of all this change, loss, and unwelcome newness, the hymn teaches us to look to God, "O Thou who changest not."

Indeed, "I need thy presence every passing hour." Isaac Bashevis Singer wryly wrote, "I only pray when I am in trouble. But I am in trouble all the time." Jesus told us to become like children, and if this means anything at all it reminds us that we are as dependent upon God as little children are upon their parents.

The final stanza is haunting. "Hold thou thy cross before my closing eyes." What is the first thing we see after birth? Most likely, it is our mothers, who bore us in agony and gave us life. What is the last thing we see? We hope it might be family, our children perhaps. The hymn asks to see the cross, the death of our Lord, God become one with us in our mortality. What comfort, what profound company we keep in the hour of death.

Have you pondered the cross, not merely as a piece of wood on which Christ dangled, but as a road sign pointing not left or right or north or south but up toward God?

Maundy Thursday

Handle Things Unseen

$\mathcal{C}$andidates for ordination and young people making their way through confirmation are asked, "What is the meaning of Holy Communion?" We might answer with some theological jargon. Seminarians learn how our greatest church leaders debated the meaning of the Lord's Supper in ferocious, shrill, violent ways— and they shudder.

Maybe the truth is simpler yet more miraculous than the Catholic doctrine of transubstantiation. We believe that when we stand in line and make our way forward to the Lord's table, we inexplicably but surely find ourselves in that upper room where Jesus first celebrated the Supper. He said, "Do this in remembrance of me," but the hidden invitation to those of us living in his future is, "Join us in this very room."

Conveyed into that upper room, we are privileged to sing with the disciples, "Here, O my Lord, I see thee face to face." They saw Jesus' face just hours before it would be bruised and bloodied. His face was full of love, but something ominous, sad, and agonizing was evident in his eyes, gestures, and words. He picked up a loaf of bread, looking closely enough as he tore it in two to catch a harrowing glimpse of what would soon happen to his own flesh. He peered into that cup of red wine and shivered over its visual similarity to the blood that would flow from his wounds. This is my body. This is my blood.

And he handed it to them, as the minister now hands bread and wine to us. "Here would I touch and handle things unseen." You don't have to subscribe to the doctrine of transubstantiation to believe that, when the piece of bread (or the round wafer) is pressed into your palm, you are handling something holy; you are holding unseen grace. It looks and feels and tastes like bread. But somehow, mystically, it's different; it's more; it's Jesus, unseen, but there tangibly. You sip the wine. It tastes like wine, going down smoothly where you can't see it anymore, and somehow Jesus has done it again: He's gotten inside you, and he'll be in you when you're back at home.

At my church we sing as we stand in line to receive Communion. How often in life do we sing with other people? The Gospels tell us Jesus and the disciples sang. We know what they sang because it was Passover. They sang psalms, like 113, 116, 118, with phrases that fit profoundly with that very night: "Who is like the LORD, who lifts up the needy to sit with princes," "I will lift up the cup of salvation," "Precious in the eyes of the LORD is the death of his saints," "This is the day the LORD has made," and "The stone the builders rejected has become the cornerstone." I try to imagine what their voices sounded like. Did Jesus lead? Did anyone harmonize? Who had the strong voice? Who were tenors or basses? In that stone room, how haunting was the reverberation, the lingering of the tones after they'd paused? Did they recall departed loved ones with whom they'd celebrated Passovers as children?

We sing, "Here would I feed upon the bread of God, here drink with thee the royal wine of heaven." Think of your parents and your grandparents who dragged you to worship, who guided you forward to do what you didn't understand. By the same miracle that transports us in time and space to the upper room with Jesus and his disciples, we are united with those we've loved and lost—saints over the centuries—at that same table.

As a child you didn't understand, and you don't know all that much now. No worries. The first disciples barely understood—but it was enough. Austin Farrer puts it this way:

> Jesus gave his body and blood to his disciples in bread and wine. Amazed at such a token, and little understanding what they did, Peter, John and the rest reached out their hands and took their master and their God. Whatever else they knew or did not know, they knew they were committed to him . . . and that they, somehow, should live it out.[9]

I love that this hymn invites us to relish the aftertaste. "Too soon we rise; the symbols disappear; the feast, though not the love, is past and gone. The bread and wine remove; but thou art here." And here. And when we get there, it will be yet another *here* where Jesus will be.

We rise and go home. Jesus rose and plunged into the darkness of Gethsemane to pray, offer himself, be arrested, and fulfill his vocation.

Day 39

GOOD FRIDAY

O Sacred Head

*T*he Crucifixion is the center of the Bible's plot, the axis on which God's redemptive love rotates. N. T. Wright calls it "the day the revolution began."[10] Protestants are attached to notions of the "empty cross," but the Bible and the long tradition of Christian prayerfulness invite us to stop, ponder, and be mortified and moved by the crucified Jesus.

If there were no lyrics at all, the tune of "O Sacred Head, Now Wounded" would itself conjure up something profound, sorrowful, and riveting. Johann Sebastian Bach was so attached to the tune that, instead of cooking up something new, he kept inserting it here and there in his *St. Matthew Passion*, his *Christmas Oratorio*, and "Komm, du süße Todesstunde." The melody and harmonies lure us in and evoke passionate grief, but then the beauty and elegance lift our heads to hope and wonder.

We might fixate on the nails piercing Jesus' hands (or wrists, actually) and feet, or the spear gutting his side. But his head is where we see the man: his eyes shedding love even as his blood is shed, his mouth dry and muttering unforgettable words, the perspiration running down his face, and his eyebrows creased in agony. He is our head, the head of the church, the head of the body of Christ;

yet it is this head that is wounded, "with grief and shame weighed down." He had no cause for shame. It is our shame—humanity's and history's—that such a holy, perfect, loving, and beautiful One would be treated so cruelly.

Jesus' head was "scornfully surrounded with thorns, thine only crown." *Zizyphus spina christi* is a vine with long sharp thorns that grows in fields and by roadsides in Palestine. I've cut a few fronds to bring home. Every time, no matter how careful I am, I get stuck by a spine. It hurts—and the hurt lingers for two or three days because the thorn has a toxicity that leaves you itching, inflamed, and with pain. When I imagine a few dozen of those prickly, mean thorns pressed into Jesus' brow, I shudder.

If we gaze at that sacred head, are we shamed or delighted, stricken or honored? The answer is "yes." This ancient hymn includes all these moods. "What thou my Lord hast suffered was all for sinners' gain: mine, mine was the transgression, but thine the deadly pain." The "mine" gets repeated, not just to make the meter work, but to remind us that we are confessing and owning doubly that our sin, the sin of each of us, put Jesus there.

"Look on me with thy favor." Does Jesus look on us with favor? His eyes looked out and saw with favor his blessed mother and his beloved disciple whom he charged to care for her. He saw the clueless soldiers and forgave them. He looked at the victim next to him and promised him paradise. He looks on us with a harrowing, surprising, tender favor. No greater favor could be envisioned.

"What language shall I borrow to thank thee, dearest friend?" At the birth of your child, at the death of your spouse, at any moment that is beautiful or horrific, there are no words. We say something inadequate, or we just sigh. What we need in this hour is a friend who doesn't have to say a word but just clutches us in quiet, firm tenderness. Jesus is that friend, our dearest friend. I love the way Mary cradles her precious son's head in Michelangelo's *Pietà*, just as she did when he was born. We too are invited to hold him, gingerly, hesitantly but then with all the love we can muster to cradle that sacred head, the very mind and heart of God—praying, or just speaking to him: "O make me thine forever . . . Lord, let me never, never outlive my love to thee."

Were You There?

$\mathcal{T}$rying to absorb, deflect, or cope with medical questioning about what must have caused her husband's death, Joan Didion kept wanting to blurt out, "Were you there?" She didn't need to "review the circumstances of the death." Why? Because she was there.[11]

A plaintive old hymn asks, "Were you there?" *Where?* "When they crucified my Lord," "when they nailed him to the tree," "when they pierced him in the side," "when the sun refused to shine," "when they laid him in the tomb." None of us were, although the Gospels, centuries of prayers, hymns, and sermons have done their best to take us to that very place, those unspeakably grievous events of Good Friday.

This hymn would have been fitting for the first Holy Saturday. What a bleak day that must have been. Those who loved Jesus were numb with grief and guilt. Their teacher and healer had been gruesomely executed, yet most of them had been too scared to stick around. Only a few lingered at the cross. Jesus' other closest friends only heard about it the way we hear about it. "Were you there?" No —but then again, yes. Trying to stave of bitter disappointment and disillusionment, they all hung their heads.

Alan Lewis calls Holy Saturday "a *significant* zero, a *pregnant* emptiness, a silent nothing which says *everything*."[12] We live our lives—don't we?—in between, like Holy Saturday. Talk to a widow whose husband died of cancer last year. She has seen Good Friday. She believes in the Easter resurrection she is pretty certain is coming, but for now she is in between.

God could have raised Jesus immediately or levitated him directly from the cross into heaven. But God waited. God did nothing for a time. God, being the kind of God we know and love, knew we would experience life and loss in just this way. We cling to hope. But the waiting can be a silent nothing. And so we wait. We live in between.

C. S. Lewis shared the grief he felt when his wife, Joy, died:

> No one ever told me that grief felt so like fear. I am not afraid, but the sensation is like being afraid. The same fluttering in the stomach, the same restlessness, the yawning. I keep on swallowing. At other times it feels like being mildly drunk, or concussed. There is a sort of invisible blanket between the world and me. I find it hard to take in what anyone says. Or perhaps, hard to want to take it in. It is so uninteresting.[13]

Our hymn spends most of its time on a long, moaning sound that barely qualifies as a word: "Oh . . . oh . . . oh." And we "tremble, tremble, tremble." Musically, by not peppering us with multiple words, the hymn sounds like we feel. The ache, the inarticulate inability to say or do anything, this anguished "Oh" draws our minds toward what I count as Paul's single greatest gift to us in all of his letters. After his insight that "the sufferings of this present time" are the whole creation "groaning in labor pains," he offers the most profound mercy: "The Spirit helps us in our weakness; for we do not know how to pray as we ought, but that very Spirit intercedes with sighs too deep for words" (Rom. 8:18-26). When there are no words, when you almost cry out, "Were you there?" When one despairing sigh after another sagging groan is exhaled from your soul, it's not despair; it is the Spirit praying in you, for you, and with you. It is the prayer God loves: the trembling "Oh . . . oh . . . oh" of Holy Saturday.

Love's Redeeming Work

HYMNS OF EASTER

*D*o congregations sing their best on Easter or Christmas Eve? These two high holy moments are the massive supports of the bridge from our lives into God's heart. God didn't hover forever aloof in the heavens, just looking down. No, God *came* down. God became one of us. God was and is with us. To complete that Christmas mission, Jesus held nothing back and embraced and experienced our mortality—the crushing of life itself—only to be raised to redeem human life and all of creation. No wonder we sing songs of triumph and tenderness.

Easter Sunday

Soar We Now

$\mathcal{A}$s a clergyperson, I will forever feel this curious ambivalence about Easter morning. It's Easter! Yet it's crowded, people are jockeying to save seats, people I've not seen since Christmas materialize, and flowers and photos seem more important than our worship. But then for me it's all redeemed when the organist, brass, and percussion strike up the opening of "Christ the Lord Is Risen Today." I know it's coming, but my knees buckle a little, and I try to choke back the tears I sense welling up. There are tears of joy. There are also tears of sorrow for those who used to join us Easter Sunday morning but are no more.

Still we realize quite a multitude beyond the crowd in the room is joining us in praise: "Sons of men and angels say . . . Sing, ye heavens and earth reply." Charles Wesley's antiquated language and worldview misses the intended inclusion of women, but he did understand that Easter isn't merely humanity gaining entrance into heaven. He saw that the whole earth is caught up in the redemption. "Love's redeeming work" is about the restoration of the entirety of God's creation.

Yes, there are forces still at work battling against life. But "Death in vain forbids him rise," reminding us of the detail of soldiers Pilate posted at Jesus' tomb to ensure he stayed in there. It is futile trying to box in the living God. Wesley's hymn shares Paul's sarcastic mockery of death: "Where, O death, is now thy sting?" "Where's thy victory, boasting grave?" We're allowed this moment of cocky jubilation at the expense of what otherwise would be our most insidious foe.

My favorite part of the hymn is the fourth stanza. I love the thought, and also that our sopranos punctuate the moment with a thrilling descant to unspeakably high notes: "Soar we now where Christ has led . . . Ours the cross, the grave, the skies." We plodding, earth-bound people just don't think in such elevated ways all that often—even in church.

The nineteenth-century Danish philosopher Søren Kierkegaard devised a parable about church for geese. Every Sunday the geese waddled into the sanctuary. A gander preached on "the glorious destiny of geese, of the noble end for which their maker had created them," namely "to use their wings to fly away to distant pastures." The geese all clucked with glee. But when the service ended, "they all waddled home, only to meet again next Sunday and waddle off home again." Over time, of course, they "grew fat, plump and delicious"—and got eaten.

Kierkegaard explained his parable:

> We too have wings, we have imagination, intended to help us actually rise aloft. But we play, allow our imagination to amuse itself in an hour of Sunday daydreaming. In reality, however, we stay right where we are—and on Monday regard it as proof that God's grace gets us plump, fat, delicate. That is, we accumulate money, get to be a somebody in the world, beget children, become successful, and so forth.[1]

Isn't it our greatest plight that we say we believe in the resurrection—we worship on Easter—and yet waddle around as if nothing has changed? It's not enough to wait to soar up from the grave after death. We sing "Soar we now." Now.

And it should not be missed that the verb "soar" has a connotation of nobility. It's not just going way up but doing so in a majestic way. And there is another hint in the word that the bird that soars does so without flapping its wings. So high, so grand, so sublime is this soaring; it is almost effortless, as if resting loftily above it all. I wonder what Jesus felt in his body the morning of Easter. Did he feel lighter?

I wonder if—after the exhaustion of Holy Week—Jesus' mind drifted to words he would have learned from his mother and heard in synagogue: "Why do you say . . . O Israel, 'My way is hid from the LORD, and my right is disregarded by my God'? Have you not known? Have you not heard? The LORD is the everlasting God, the Creator of the ends of the earth. He does not faint or grow weary. . . . Even youths shall faint and be weary, and young men shall fall exhausted; but they who wait for the LORD shall renew their strength, they shall mount up with wings like eagles, they shall run and not be weary, they shall walk and not faint" (Isa. 40:27-31, RSV).

Easter Monday

I Come to the Garden Alone

*W*hat can we make of an old hymn that was popularized on Billy Sunday's revival circuit and then recorded by Roy Rogers and Dale Evans, Tennessee Ernie Ford, Elvis Presley, Mahalia Jackson, Loretta Lynn, and the Avett Brothers? Despite being dropped from the Methodist hymnal of 1964, it withstood being so dissed and remained a top ten favorite until it was restored in the 1989 Methodist hymnal. Its origin? Back in 1912, C. Austin Miles, an amateur photographer, was pondering John 20 while waiting for some film to develop.

> As I read it that day, I seemed to be part of the scene. . . . I seemed to be standing at the entrance of a garden, looking down a gently winding path, shaded by olive branches. A woman in white, with head bowed, hand clasping her throat as if to choke back her sobs, walked slowly into the shadows . . . Turning herself, she saw Jesus standing; so did I . . . Under the inspiration of this vision I wrote as quickly as the words would be formed the poem exactly as it has since appeared. That same evening I wrote the music.[2]

"I come to the garden alone." The "I" is Mary Magdalene. Mary and Jesus met up on Easter Sunday. The Gospels don't say that they met in a garden, but John 20:15 tells us Mary mistook Jesus for the gardener. This makes me think of *Being There,* the brilliant Peter Sellers film from 1979 about mistaken identity. Chance the gardener is mistaken for an upper-class businessman, Chauncey Gardiner, and people leap to absurd conclusions, finding his simple-minded sayings about gardening to be the most profound wisdom. Did people leap to ridiculous conclusions about Jesus? Mary was downright sure he was dead: She couldn't recognize him because her sorrow was so strong and her belief that the dead stay dead was so solid. Then she heard her name and was sure he was alive.

The garden envisioned in the hymn is more verdant than the vicinity of Jesus' tomb, which would have been a rocky, uncultivated patch of earth. "The dew is still on the roses" is a bit romantic, as is the idea of Jesus' voice being "so sweet the birds hush their singing." Jesus did speak to Mary, calling her by name. How lovely. God knows and addresses all of us by name. Isaiah 49:16 tantalizingly suggests that your name is tattooed on the palm of God's hand—as is mine and as was Mary's.

The rhythm of "And he walks with me and he talks with me" feels like we are skipping along with him. Mary's encounter was brief. She impulsively and understandably reached out to embrace him, but he pushed back: "Do not cling to me." Then he was gone, but not really gone. The hymn owns that we feel the pangs of separation and also Jesus' lingering presence after his departure. He bids us go, but once we do go back out into the world, we can, along with Mary, testify that he still "walks with me and he talks with me."

The sweetness of the hymn is a bit at odds with the resurrection accounts in the Gospels, where the first witnesses are frightened and dumbstruck and scurry off with the news, trembling in awe and uncertainty. The hymn does remind us that gaining a ticket to heaven when we die is not the main point of the resurrection. The presence of the Lord continues after the resurrection days are over. Jesus pledged to the disciples at the Last Supper that he would send the Spirit to comfort, challenge, enlighten, and be his presence going forward. This is the plot of the Gospels: Jesus is raised; therefore, you are forgiven.

Epilogue

Something God Alone Can See

The origin of hymns and the life stories of composers usually aren't things I obsess over, maybe in the same way I enjoy watching ballplayers or listening to music without needing to know so much about a quarterback's love life or a guitarist's partying. But sometimes circumstances within which a hymn was birthed can help us to overhear a deeper resonance and some untapped emotion.

Natalie Sleeth began publishing anthems in the late 1960s and wound up conceiving more than two hundred anthems for choirs. "In the Bulb There Is a Flower," a choral piece we know as the "Hymn of Promise," sprang from a season in the mid-1980s when she was "pondering ideas of life, death, spring, winter, Good Friday and Easter," and also T. S. Eliot's intriguing poetic line, "In my beginning is my end,"[1] which she cleverly reversed to "In our end is our beginning." The words and music she wrote were simple, eloquent, and beautiful.

And then, just a few days after putting the finishing touches on it, her husband, Ronald (a professor of preaching), was diagnosed with a terminal malignancy. When he heard her play the anthem for him, he asked that it be sung as a hymn at his funeral. So it was. He was only sixty-three. She lived seven more years, dying at age sixty-one. I've sung it now at enough funerals of people I've loved that I get little choked up and teary any time I hear it.

Superficially, the hymn is about natural beauty. But what did Sleeth select from the world of nature? Just as the apostle Paul tried to explain the resurrection of the body by pointing to the way seed falls into the ground, Sleeth draws our attention to a flower bulb, an apple seed, a cocoon. If an alien arrived from another planet and picked up a bulb or a cocoon, it would probably toss it aside as of no use. If someone said it will become a fragrant flower or a beautiful butterfly, the alien would scoff. The bulb, seed, and cocoon persuade us that, yes, we do know something of surprise, of unanticipated new life.

So she leads us then to recall that a cold winter eventually yields to the warmth of spring. Silence can be deafening for the one who grieves. Can the hollow silence become holy stillness? Can a song transform the empty space into a holy place? The dawn does dawn after all. That apple seed really is transformed, if you wait long enough, into a tall, sturdy tree producing fruit for us to eat.

When Sleeth died at age sixty-one, she ceased being productive. But her work is still bearing much fruit. Isn't this the goal for all of us? We only produce for a brief time. But our love, our words, and our being can still be fruitful even long after we are gone.

When we bury our dead, even if we purchase a pretty casket or a velvety box for the columbarium, the body isn't much to behold, with no life in it. God's surprise, God's gift, is entirely hidden from us—and yet it is surely there. It's "something God alone can see." God, even in the hour of death, can already see our redeemed, eternal life of joy, light, and love. And so ours is to hope.

The hymn captures how grief works. When we have no words, when we shrink back in the quiet, "there's a song in every silence." I continue to be impressed by brave families who stand in our sanctuary and defy death by raising their voices in hymns. Their loved one is now all memory, but "from the past will come the future, what it holds, a mystery." We do not know what will happen next; we aren't entirely sure about the shape of a reunion or a regathering to come. It's "something God alone can see."

The Eliot line makes us dizzy with paradox—and that is how hope works. It's not the logic, it's not our control, and it's certainly nothing automatic or even natural. "In our end is our beginning; in our time, infinity; in our life, eternity; in our death, a resurrection"—and this victory is "something God alone can see." It's "unrevealed until its season." In the meantime, in this season, ours is to grieve, sing, and hope.

Leader's Guide

$\mathcal{W}$elcome to the leader's guide for *Unrevealed Until Its Season*. Below you will find reflection material that correlates with each week of Lent. Each section includes a prayer, a series of conversation starters, a closing prayer, and a preview question for the next week. As you gather each week, invite the group to light a candle before the opening prayer.

These questions and prompts are an invitation into conversation and deeper meaning. Use them in whatever way the group needs. If you only get through one prompt during your allotted time, that is okay. If you use all of the prompts, that is also okay. Feel free to follow the thread of conversation and let the hymns guide your wandering.

This book follows a daily reading schedule, and this reflection material is based on the daily readings. The study will work best if participants read the book throughout the week prior to meeting.

As the leader, provide hymnals or printed words to the hymns you will focus on each week. If you have access to a piano or other instrument (and someone in your group knows how to play!), meet in a room where you can play along with the participants who are singing. Another option is to listen to the hymns by looking them up online and playing them on your laptop or phone speakers. Invite participants to bring a copy of their book and a journal and pen if they would like to take notes.

Unrevealed Until Its Season offers readers a meaningful opportunity to reflect on each week of Lent. May you be comforted by these hymns as you journey with Christ to the cross.

First Week in Lent
Merciful and Mighty: Hymns Praising God

Materials

Hymnals or copies of "Here I Am, Lord," journals or loose paper, and pens (optional: colored pencils, markers, crayons, etc.)

Opening Prayer

Holy God, you love us beyond comprehension. We are in awe of your holiness, presence, and greatness. We admit that we allow our insecurities to freeze us. Help us remember that you simply ask us to show up to say, "Here I am." Amen.

Hymn

"Here I Am, Lord"

Conversation Starters

"'Holy, Holy, Holy' isn't about our feelings (or even us!) at all. It's about God. This hymn expresses awe. Being in awe is the gift of worship you won't stumble upon anywhere else in your life" (24).

> *Where and when do you feel most in awe? How do you express feelings of awe?*

"What is the rousing reply we're drawn into making with Isaiah through this hymn? 'Here I am, Lord . . . I have heard you calling in the night; I will go Lord . . . I will hold your people in my heart.' Don't sing this unless you're seriously ready for your routine life and your accustomed ways to be interrupted" (28).

> *What thoughts and feelings arise as you read these words? What holds you back from offering your life to God in this*

way? Describe what it would be like for you to hear God's call and follow.

"We will never exaggerate when we speak of God's amazing greatness. Our most spectacular, eloquent words, songs, and actions will be embarrassingly modest, falling far short of how great God is. When I think of this hymn and of God's greatness, I recall the times I've heard it sung in faraway places and in different languages" (33).

Pause for a minute of silence to consider your own experiences of God's greatness. Where were you? How old were you? What did it feel like? What did you hear? Were you alone or with others? What verbs, nouns, and adjectives would you use to describe the moment? Write or draw whatever you are thinking about. Share it with the group when the leader invites discussion.

"We know this restless sense of yearning for home but never quite settling in. . . . God seems to have fashioned us with this hankering for home and also with the gnawing sensation that we're never quite there" (37).

Where have you felt most at home? Describe a time when you felt at peace in a place. What was missing? What felt complete?

"When I am a thankful person, when I am in the act of expressing gratitude, I cannot feel anxious. If we look back with gratitude, then we naturally look forward with hope. It is the antithesis of looking back with guilt or regret, which leaves you stuck looking forward with nothing but anxiety and fear" (40-41).

How does this excerpt sit with you? Do you instinctively approach life with a posture of gratitude? Or do guilt and

regret creep into your mind more often than you would like?
How might you creatively integrate moments of gratitude into
your daily life? What would it look like for gratitude to be
a spiritual practice? Take time to brainstorm ideas with the
group.

Closing Prayer

Holy, Holy, Holy One,
We praise you with our singing.
We praise you with our dancing.
We praise you with our quiet hearts.
We praise you with our steady breath.
We want to follow your call.
Help us as we take brave steps into the future.
Open our eyes as you open our hearts.
Amen.

For Next Week

As you read next week, keep this quote in mind: "God's extravagance is absurd. It's like manna, a little, just enough. But then it's plenty, way more than enough. When Jesus broke the bread beside the sea, he got carried away. Thousands ate plenty and had basketfuls left over. 'Break thou the bread of life,' we pray—and we'd best brace ourselves. An abundance of bread, truth, holiness, love, mercy, and hope are about to burst forth from the broken place" (54).

Second Week in Lent
Beautiful Savior: Hymns About Jesus

Materials

Hymnals or copies of "What a Friend We Have in Jesus," journals or loose paper, and pens (optional: colored pencils, markers, crayons, etc.)

Opening Prayer

Jesus our friend,
Your mercy is unending.
You care for those we ignore.
You notice those we regard as invisible.
Your unending love quenches our thirst and washes us clean.
Teach us to care and to notice in the way you do.
Make our hearts more merciful.
In the midst of the rough seas of life, we long for your friendship.
Come, Lord Jesus, come.

Hymn

"What a Friend We Have in Jesus"

Conversation Starters

"'Fairest Lord Jesus' simply notices and then extols the beauty of Jesus. . . . People dropped everything to follow him. They risked and lost their lives for him, so great was their devotion to him" (47).

Following Jesus isn't always the path of least resistance. What have you risked following Jesus? What is it about Jesus that makes this risk worth it?

"Why are we so drawn to water? Is it because we began our lives in the water of our mother's womb? Is it that our bodies are mostly water? Water quenches thirst, washes us clean, and is simply beautiful to behold. And it is not entirely safe. How many of the Gospel stories feature the disciples being terrified on that very lake? Doesn't the water symbolize our inevitable humility, defying our grossly overrated ability to manage things?" (50).

Take a moment to remember your baptism. If you have not been baptized, think of a transforming moment when you felt close to God. Write down a few notes describing the experience. How did baptism or this transforming moment change your life?

"But then Jesus shifted the topic from bread to the bread of life— as in the will of God, as in not living by bread alone but by every word from the mouth of the Lord, as in following him (see John 6:35-40)" (53).

Consider the phrase "bread of life." What does it mean to you? How do you sustain your body? How do you sustain your spirit?

"The image of Jesus as friend is even more profound than we might imagine" (55).

Describe the various qualities of a good friend. How does your relationship with Jesus change if you think of him as a friend? How might this perspective affect the way you pray?

"If we ponder the mercy and miracle that Jesus loved us when we'd made ourselves strangers to him, then loving him in return by loving the stranger is a simple reflex of mercy" (66).

Share with the group some examples of times when Jesus loved
the stranger, the least of these, or those who are overlooked.
What do these stories have in common? How do they differ?
What does loving the stranger look like in your everyday life?

Closing Prayer

Jesus, Bread of Life,

You give your body so that we might have eternal life.

Blessed.

Broken.

Poured.

Your love for us is eternal.

Forgive us when we stray from your will.

Guide us as we follow you, pouring out love to everyone we encounter.

Open our eyes as you open our hearts.

Amen.

For Next Week

As you read next week's chapters, reflect on this quote: "Sin is visible when we see ourselves in the light of Jesus' life—the life upon which this past week's hymns have reflected. The gap between our lives and Jesus' words, actions, and being is the space we desperately want bridged; this is the healing we need but cannot manufacture, and this is the great grief of our soul" (67).

Third Week in Lent
Prone to Wander: HYMNS OF FORGIVENESS

Materials

Hymnals or copies of "Come, Thou Fount of Every Blessing," journals or loose paper, and pens (optional: colored pencils, markers, crayons, etc.)

Opening Prayer

Holy God, though we are prone to wander, we are grateful that you always shepherd us back into the flock. We come to you with open hands and open hearts, asking for forgiveness and trusting that, though we often fall short, you love each of us as we are. Forgive us, we pray. Amen.

Hymn

"Come, Thou Fount of Every Blessing"

Conversation Starters

"It is so lovely when a hymn bridges that gulf between human brokenness and the divine presence. 'Come, Thou Fount of Every Blessing' succeeds marvelously, partly due to its tune and harmonies" (68).

Describe an experience or moment that bridged the gulf between human brokenness and the divine presence.

"God loves you and all of us—the soldiers gambling for his clothing, the thief on the cross next to him, and the guy who got on your nerves today—that much. Just as I am, I ponder this marvel. Just as I am, I soak in the glory of this humbling truth" (75).

Do you find it easy or difficult to live as if God loves you just the way you are? What parts of yourself do you attempt to polish and clean up—as if editing and filtering a photo—when you approach God?

"But God's love is overwhelmingly and delightfully so much greater, more marvelous, and more extensive than all the love we might imagine woven together. Yet it's accessible; it's personal and as small as a hug or a young child nestled in your lap: 'Joy of heaven to earth come down.' Indeed, God made a 'humble dwelling' down here in Bethlehem when Jesus was born" (77).

We often look for evidence of God's love in grand, striking, or majestic moments. What would we find if we looked for God's love in small spaces? In the tiny? In the humble? Describe a time you felt the love of God in a small moment.

"I might be in a sanctuary with a few dozen others. But at that moment, dozens of dozens of others are praising in churches nearby. If we think of the churches across the globe and God's people throughout time, the numbers begin to stagger the mind." (82)

If you could witness churches across the globe and all the saints above gathered into one scene singing praises to God, what hymn would you want them to sing? What would this experience feel like? Imagine how you would feel. Imagine what you would see and hear.

"All really will be well. In the moment of hearing it, saying it, or singing it, I believe" (84).

What beliefs do you have that, in hearing it or singing it, have become more real to you? How would you describe the impact that singing or listening to hymns has on your faith?

Closing Prayer

Forgiving God,

We look for you in sweeping mountain vista scenes, loud claps of thunder, and powerful ocean waves. We look for you in miraculous moments and grand gestures of love and reconciliation. Remind us also to see you in tiny seeds that have yet to push through the dirt and in hummingbirds flitting by.

Remind us to see your love in small acts of graciousness, humble and fleeting moments of kindness.

Open our eyes as you open our hearts.

Amen.

For Next Week

"Faith is 'the conviction of things not seen' (Heb. 11:1)—but then they are seen by the eyes of faith. Jesus' favorite miracle seemed to be healing the blind; there's something in this about those who thought they could see but couldn't really" (89).

Fourth Week in Lent
Thy Presence My Light: HYMNS OF VISION

Materials

Hymnals or copies of "Be Thou My Vision" and "His Eye Is on the Sparrow," journals or loose paper, and pens (optional: colored pencils, markers, crayons, etc.)

Opening Prayer

Holy God,

We praise you with our minds.

We praise you with our hearts.

We praise you with our lives.
We praise you with our very breath.
Amen.

Hymns

"Be Thou My Vision" and "His Eye Is on the Sparrow"

Conversation Starters

"[Be Thou My Vision] asks for a peculiar vision—that the Lord will not merely help or correct my vision but rather 'Be thou my vision, O Lord.' You be my eyes" (90).

Imagine that there are glasses you can put on that give you Jesus' eyes. How does your perspective change? What is different about how you see the world? How would this vision change your actions?

"Hymns extol God's goodness and bind the individual's soul to God. Hymns also can have an impact on society, on us as people together, and on the church's work out in the world" (96).

Make a list of a few hymns that have changed society. If it helps, flip through a hymnal as you do this. Share with the group why you think the hymns you selected have impacted society.

"The church's task isn't to pass judgment, condemn, or hunker down behind our secure walls. We dream of becoming a safe place for everyone. For that to happen, we have to get busy doing what Jesus told us to do: creating justice, discovering and spreading joy, and making peace instead of division. The hymn says this is God's joy too! 'God will delight when we are creators of justice and joy'" (97).

In order to become a safe place for everyone, we must create justice, discover and spread joy, and make peace. How might this vision of God's joy become our own vision for joy? What is one thing you can do this week that works toward this goal?

"What's so lovely about the hymn ['His Eye Is on the Sparrow'] is that it doesn't pledge or expect a quick fix or any fix at all. It's not that God will do what I ask or that God will repair everything tomorrow. It's simply that God cares. God sees" (100).

Knowing that God cares, what do you bring before God this week?

"While we have breath, we praise the Lord—in our minds, hearts, and lives" (103).

What does it look like to praise God in your daily life?

Closing Prayer

O Lord, be our vision.
Help us to create justice, discover and spread joy, and make peace.
Illuminate our gifts as we set ourselves to do your work.
Open our eyes as you open our hearts.
Amen.

For Next Week

"God created beauty out there, partly just showing off, partly luring us into the beauty that is the heart and mind of God. From nature we learn how to be our natural, God-imaged selves" (111). As you reflect on the readings this coming week, take time to slow down, notice, and make note of the beauty God creates.

Fifth Week in Lent
With Joy Surround You: HYMNS OF BEAUTY

Materials

Hymnals or copies of "All Creatures of Our God and King," journals or loose paper, and pens (optional: colored pencils, markers, crayons, etc.)

Opening Prayer

Creating God,

You create the stars in the sky, the flowers of the field, and the fish in the sea. You create our lives to live out love. You sustain us when the world feels too heavy. You always create new mornings, and for that we give thanks.

Amen.

Hymn

"All Creatures of our God and King"

Conversation Starters

"Van Dyke's most eloquent image might be 'Hearts unfold like flowers before Thee.' Watch flowers. Don't just glance at them. Give it some time. Flowers take time. They don't sprout up in a jiffy. Gardeners understand that the cultivation and care of flowers requires patience, vigilance, and tenderness. The human heart yearns for a Lord and for faithful friends who are patient, vigilant, and tender. Flowers are fragile. That is their wonder. We know that a gust of wind, a scurrying squirrel, or a hard rain might damage them. They are transient like us, and yet they are lovely. Lent is about our transient mortality—which is our beauty too" (113).

*Have you ever cared for flowers? Describe the process of grow-
ing a flower from seed to bloom. What conditions must exist
for a flower to grow properly? What does a flower need for the
journey of growth? In what ways is this process similar to how
our own human hearts yearn for the Lord?*

"It's as if God created the world—morning and evening, sun rising, setting, darkness, and then the dawn—in imitation of Easter,
which did dawn on people in the morning. Each morning is a
little Easter, a new beginning even for the most encrusted, stuck,
pessimistic among us. The sun has risen. Again. What to do with
another day? It's just a day. And yet my lifetime is nothing but a
day, another day, a whole bunch of days" (116).

*It is a comfort that, whatever has happened in a day, we can
trust that night comes and a new morning will dawn. Think
of a time that this truth has helped you through a hard season.
What are the spiritual practices that sustain you during hard
times?*

"Gratitude seems to dawn on us quite naturally when something
extraordinary happens. . . . Gratitude looks around and notices
what is ever-present. . . . Gratitude looks around and looks back,
not in regret or grief but seeing what has been a blessing. . . . And
then gratitude looks forward" (122).

*Make three lists and label them Past, Present, and Future.
Under these headings, write or draw what you are grateful
for in the past, present, and future. After the group has had
enough time to reflect, share what you have listed. Consider
incorporating the practice of keeping a gratitude journal into
your spiritual life.*

"The hymn ['All Creatures of Our God and King'] invites us—not just while singing but all the time—to develop eyes and ears to perceive beauty where many miss it" (124).

The "For Next Week" note from last week asked readers to pay attention to God's created beauty. What was it like to go through the week with a focus on noticing creation? What did you see? Describe the experience to the group.

"Made of dust, we return to dust. We are of the earth, one with nature. Lent is the peaceful realization of our mortality" (130).

Mortality is not a topic that most people like to dwell on and talk about. Do you typically experience Lent as the peaceful realization of your mortality? Or is the realization more sudden? What is it like to travel through a six-week season that is focused on mortality?

Closing Prayer

Holy God,
You form us out of love and dust. We return to you as love and dust. Help us to slow down and pay attention to the beauty of your creation that is all around us.
Open our eyes as you open our hearts.
Amen.

For Next Week

"Day by day, we ponder what Jesus did—his courage, his commitment, his immense compassion—and how the events of a single week from so long ago still resonate with us today" (133). As you move through Holy Week, take time to ponder what Jesus did, his courage, his commitment, and his immense compassion.

Sixth Week in Lent
Stony the Road: HYMNS OF HOLY WEEK

Materials

Hymnals or copies of "O Sacred Head, Now Wounded," journals or loose paper, and pens (optional: colored pencils, markers, crayons, etc.)

Opening Prayer

Jesus, your death and resurrection are the culmination of the work of many prophets before you. Your victory over death redeems us and invites us into God's work in the world. Teach us to love as you love.

Amen.

Hymn

"O Sacred Head, Now Wounded"

Conversation Starters

"Jesus acted. He stepped boldly into the long tradition of prophetic action in God's name—from Moses striding into the courts of Pharaoh to Ezekiel's symbolic cutting of his hair and beard. That tradition has gone on. The labor for God's goodness in the real world is long and painful, requiring resilience and uncompromising hope" (138).

> *How have you stepped boldly into prophetic action? How might you continue that work into the future?*

"Hymns can help us live into the already/not yet truths of Christian existence. We sing 'Victory in Jesus,' but that victory is not yet fully won. Jesus died to redeem the world, but clearly it is far from redeemed" (138).

What hymns echo in your thoughts as you consider living into the already/not yet truths of the Christian existence?

"That's God, this fellowship of three. Just as the Emmaus story invites you the reader to join the threesome of Jesus and the other two, God's holy club invites you to pull up a chair on that open fourth side of the table" (143).

In this Holy Week, imagine you are pulling up a chair to the fourth side of this table. What questions do you ask? What is the conversation like?

"We believe that when we stand in line and make our way forward to the Lord's table, we inexplicably but surely find ourselves in that upper room where Jesus first celebrated the Supper" (146).

Think about the first time you took Communion. Think about an impactful time that you took Communion. Describe these experiences to the group. What is the meaning of Holy Communion to you?

"What language shall I borrow to thank thee, dearest friend?" (150).

What language could we use to thank Jesus? Does such language exist? How else can we thank Jesus?

"We live our lives—don't we?—in between, like Holy Saturday. Talk to a widow whose husband died of cancer last year. She has seen Good Friday. She believes in the Easter resurrection she is pretty certain is coming, but for now, she is in between" (152-53).

Reflect on what it means to be in between. How does it feel?
What is it like to be on the other side of Good Friday while
anticipating Easter?

Closing Prayer

O Sacred Head, now wounded, we grieve as we witness your death.
In the darkness of Good Friday, we wait for the light dawning on
Easter morning.
Open our eyes as you open our hearts.
Amen.

For Next Week

"To complete that Christmas mission, Jesus held nothing back and
embraced and experienced our mortality—the crushing of life
itself—only to be raised to redeem human life and all of creation.
No wonder we sing songs of triumph and tenderness" (155). As you
look forward to the coming Easter morning, reflect with anticipation on the songs that will be raised with triumph and tenderness.

Easter
Love's Redeeming Work: HYMNS OF EASTER

Materials

Hymnals or copies of "Christ the Lord Is Risen Today"

Opening Prayer *(to be read responsively)*

Christ is risen!
Alleluia!
Christ is risen!
Alleluia!

Christ is risen!
Alleluia!
Amen.

Hymn

"Christ the Lord Is Risen Today"

Conversation Starters

"As a clergyperson, I will forever feel this curious ambivalence about Easter morning. It's Easter! Yet it's crowded, people are jockeying to save seats, people I've not seen since Christmas materialize, and flowers and photos seem more important than our worship. But then for me it's all redeemed when the organist, brass, and percussion strike up the opening of 'Christ the Lord Is Risen Today.' I know it's coming, but my knees buckle a little, and I try to choke back the tears I sense welling up. There are tears of joy. There are also tears of sorrow for those who used to join us Easter Sunday morning but are no more" (156).

Describe a fond Easter morning memory. What Easter traditions do you most value? What emotions accompany Easter?

"The presence of the Lord continues after the resurrection days are over. Jesus pledged to the disciples at the Last Supper that he would send the Spirit to comfort, challenge, enlighten, and be his presence going forward. This is the plot of the Gospels: Jesus is raised; therefore, you are forgiven" (161).

Jesus is raised, you are forgiven, and now the Spirit works in and through us to share love and resurrection hope to the world. Describe and discuss the evidence of the Spirit in your life as you work to share God's story of hope and love.

Closing Prayer *(to be read responsively)*

Christ the Lord is risen today.
Alleluia!
Love's redeeming work is done.
Alleluia!
Ours the cross, the grave, the skies!
Alleluia! Alleluia! Alleluia!
Amen.

Notes

Introduction

1. Albert Edward Bailey, *The Gospel in Hymns: Backgrounds and Interpretations* (New York: Charles Scribner's Sons, 1950), 405.
2. Jonathan Sacks, *Covenant and Conversation: A Weekly Reading of the Jewish Bible*, vol. 1, *Genesis: The Book of Beginnings* (New Milford, CT: Maggid Books, 2009), 188–89.
3. Stephen R. Covey, *The 7 Habits of Highly Effective People* (New York: Simon and Schuster, 1988), 98.
4. James C. Howell, *Struck from Behind: My Memories of God* (Eugene, OR: Cascade Books, 2012).
5. Robert Alter, *Genesis: Translation and Commentary* (New York: W. W. Norton, 1996), 149.
6. Eric Metaxas, *Bonhoeffer: Pastor, Martyr, Prophet, Spy* (Nashville, TN: Thomas Nelson, 2010), 361.

First Week in Lent

1. Jonathan Sacks, *Covenant and Conversation: A Weekly Reading of the Jewish Bible*, vol. 2, *Exodus: The Book of Redemption* (New Milford, CT: Maggid Books, 2010), 141.
2. Jeremy Begbie, *Resounding Truth: Christian Wisdom in the World of Music* (Grand Rapids, MI: Baker Academic, 2007), 293.
3. Richard Stearns, *The Hole in Our Gospel* (Nashville, TN: Thomas Nelson, 2009), 9.
4. Albert Edward Bailey, *The Gospel in Hymns: Backgrounds and Interpretations* (New York: Charles Scribner's Sons, 1950), 48.
5. Eddie Izzard, from his monologue "Dress to Kill."

6. James Melvin Washington, ed., *A Testament of Hope: The Essential Writings and Speeches of Martin Luther King, Jr.* (San Francisco: HarperCollins, 1986), 286.

7. Reinhold Niebuhr, *The Irony of American History* (New York: Charles Scribner's Sons, 1952), 63.

8. *Macbeth*, ed. Barbara A. Mowat and Paul Werstine (New York: Washington Square Press, 1992), 5.5.26–27.

9. William Manchester and Paul Reid, *The Last Lion: Winston Spencer Churchill: Defender of the Realm, 1940–1965* (New York: Little, Brown, 2012), 19.

10. Raymond Barfield, *Wager: Beauty, Suffering, and Being in the World* (Eugene, OR: Cascade Books, 2017), 1.

11. St. Augustine, *Confessions*, trans. Sarah Ruden (New York: Modern Library, 2017), 3.

12. Carl Sandburg, *Abraham Lincoln: The Prairie Years and the War Years* (San Diego: Harvest, 1954), 407.

13. Jad Abumrad and Shima Oliaee, "8: Neon Moss," Nov. 5, 2019, in *Dolly Parton's America*, produced by WNYC Studios, podcast, MP3 audio, 43:51, https://www.wnycstudios.org/podcasts/dolly-partons-america/episodes/neon-moss.

14. Roland H. Bainton, *Here I Stand: A Life of Martin Luther* (New York: Mentor, 1950), 266.

15. Martin E. P. Seligman, *Flourish: A Visionary New Understanding of Happiness and Well-Being* (New York: Atria, 2011), ch. 2.

16. Abraham Joshua Heschel, *The Sabbath: Its Meaning for Modern Man* (New York: Farrar, Straus and Giroux, 1951), 8.

17. Brian Doyle, *One Long River of Song: Notes on Wonder* (New York: Little, Brown, 2019), 239.

Second Week in Lent

1. Prince Myshkin is accused of saying this. See Fyodor Dostoevsky, *The Idiot*, trans. and ed. Alan Myers (New York: Oxford University Press, 1992), 402.

2. Janina Ramirez, *Julian of Norwich: A Very Brief History* (London: SPCK, 2017), 40.

3. John Navone, S. J., *Enjoying God's Beauty* (Collegeville, MN: Liturgical, 1999), 5.

4. John O'Donohue, *Beauty: The Invisible Embrace* (New York: Harper Perennial, 2004), 115.

5. James Gleick, *Isaac Newton* (New York: Vintage Books, 2003), 4.

6. Albert Edward Bailey, *The Gospel in Hymns: Backgrounds and Interpretations* (New York: Charles Scribner's Sons, 1950), 496.

7. Paul J. Wadell, C.P., *Friendship and the Moral Life* (Notre Dame, IN: University of Notre Dame Press, 1989), xiii.

8. Wadell, *Friendship and the Moral Life*, 106.

9. G. K. Chesterton, *St. Francis of Assisi* (Garden City, NJ: Image Books, 1957), 47.

10. Martin Luther King, Jr., *A Gift of Love: Sermons from "Strength To Love" and Other Preachings* (Boston: Beacon, 2012), 50.

11. Guy Gaucher, *The Story of a Life: St. Thérèse of Lisieux* (San Francisco: Harper Collins, 1987), 51, 148.

12. Roger Scruton, *Beauty: A Very Short Introduction* (New York: Oxford University Press, 2011), 61.

13. Bailey, *The Gospel in Hymns*, 119–20.

Third Week in Lent

1. Isaac Watts, *The Psalms of David* (Seattle: Pacific Publishing Studio, 2011), 21.

2. William Manchester, *The Last Lion: Winston Spencer Churchill: Visions of Glory, 1874–1932* (New York: Dell, 1983), 367.

3. Oscar Romero, *The Violence of Love*, trans. James R. Brockman, S. J. (Farmington: Plough, 1998), 29–30.

4. Paul Tillich, *The Shaking of the Foundations* (New York: Charles Scribner's Sons, 1948), 162.

5. Walter Brueggemann, *A Glad Obedience: Why and What We Sing* (Louisville, KY: Westminster John Knox, 2019), 113.

6. Albert Edward Bailey, *The Gospel in Hymns: Backgrounds and Interpretations* (New York: Charles Scribner's Sons, 1950), 97.

7. St. Augustine, *On Christian Doctrine*, trans. D. W. Robertson, Jr. (Indianapolis, IN: Bobbs-Merrill, 1958), bk. I, chs. 3–5, 22.

8. Jonathan Sacks, *Covenant and Conversation: A Weekly Reading of the Jewish Bible*, vol. 2, *Exodus: The Book of Redemption* (New Milford, CT: Maggid Books, 2010), 99.

9. Juliana of Norwich, *Revelations of Divine Love*, trans. M. L. del Mastro (Garden City, NY: Image Books, 1977), 124.

10. Robert J. Morgan, *Then Sings My Soul* (Nashville, TN: Thomas Nelson, 2003), 113.

Fourth Week in Lent

1. Robert Coles, *Dorothy Day: A Radical Devotion* (Reading, MA: Addison-Wesley, 1987), 16.

2. Quoted in "The Harvard in Thoreau," Richard Higgins, *The Harvard Gazette*, June 29, 2017, https://news.harvard.edu/gazette/story/2017/06/near-the-bicentennial-of-thoreaus-birth-a-look-at-his-harvard-years/.

3. Henry David Thoreau, *Walden and Other Writings of Henry David Thoreau*, ed. Brooks Atkinson (New York: Random House, 1992), 49.

4. Samuel Wells, *A Nazareth Manifesto: Being with God* (Malden, MA: John Wiley and Sons, 2015), 3, 11.

5. Jonathan Sacks, *Covenant and Conversation: A Weekly Reading of the Jewish Bible*, vol. 2, *Exodus: The Book of Redemption* (New Milford, CT: Maggid Books, 2010), 186.

6. Jonathan Sacks, *Covenant and Conversation: A Weekly Reading of the Jewish Bible*, vol. 1, *Genesis: The Book of Beginnings* (New Milford, CT: Maggid Books, 2009), 232.

7. Graham Greene, *The End of the Affair* (New York: Penguin Books, 1962), 110.

8. Frederick Buechner, *The Magnificent Defeat* (San Francisco: Harper and Row, 1966), 18.

9. Jim Forest, *Love Is the Measure: A Biography of Dorothy Day*, rev. ed. (Maryknoll, NY: Orbis Books, 1994), 135.

10. Walter Brueggemann, *A Glad Obedience: Why and What We Sing* (Louisville, KY: Westminster John Knox, 2019), 147.

11. Raymond Barfield, *Wager: Beauty, Suffering, and Being in the World* (Eugene, OR: Cascade Books, 2017), 72.

12. Gregory Boyle, *Barking to the Choir: The Power of Radical Kinship* (New York: Simon and Schuster, 2017), 205.

Fifth Week in Lent

1. Harvey Sachs, *The Ninth: Beethoven and the World in 1824* (New York: Random House, 2010), 3.
2. Sachs, *The Ninth*, 4.
3. Sachs, *The Ninth*, 154.
4. Arthur Miller, *After the Fall: A Play in Two Acts* (New York: Penguin Books, 1964), 3–4.
5. David J. Wolpe, *The Healer of Shattered Hearts: A Jewish View of God* (New York: Penguin Books, 1990), 105.
6. Raymond Barfield, *Wager: Beauty, Suffering, and Being in the World* (Eugene, OR: Cascade Books, 2017), 1.
7. *Francis of Assisi: Early Documents*, vol. 1, ed. Regis J. Armstrong, J. A. Wayne Hellman, and William J. Short (New York: New City, 1999), 234.
8. *Francis of Assisi: Early Documents*, vol. 3, ed. Regis J. Armstrong, J. A. Wayne Hellman, and William J. Short (New York: New City Press, 2001), 632–33.
9. Lawrence S. Cunningham, *Francis of Assisi: Performing the Gospel Life* (Grand Rapids, MI: Eerdmans, 2004), 100.
10. Donald E. Gowan, *The Bible on Forgiveness* (Eugene, OR: Pickwick, 2010), 17.
11. Cunningham, *Francis of Assisi*, 111.
12. Henri J. M. Nouwen, *The Inner Voice of Love: A Journey Through Anguish to Freedom* (New York: Image Books, 1996), 107.
13. Ernest Becker, *The Denial of Death* (New York: Free Press, 1973).

Sixth Week in Lent

1. John Lewis said this frequently. See https://www.pbs.org/show/john-lewis-get-in-the-way/.
2. Taylor Branch, *Parting the Waters: America in the King Years, 1954-63* (New York: Simon and Schuster, 1988), 149.

3. J. Christiaan Beker, *Paul the Apostle: The Triumph of God in Life and Thought* (Philadelphia: Fortress, 1980), 155.

4. David Halberstam, *The Children* (New York: Fawcett Books, 1998), 140.

5. *The Hymns of the United Methodist Hymnal: Introduction to the Hymns, Canticles, and Acts of Worship*, ed. Diana Sanchez (Nashville, TN: Abingdon, 1989), 203.

6. Mark Helprin, *Winter's Tale* (New York: Pocket Books, 1983), 211.

7. Plato, *Gorgias*, 481c, trans. W. D. Woodhead, *The Collected Dialogues of Plato*, ed. Edith Hamilton and Huntington Cairns (Princeton: Princeton University Press, 1961), 265.

8. Jonathan Sacks, *Covenant and Conversation: A Weekly Reading of the Jewish Bible*, vol. 2, *Exodus: The Book of Redemption* (New Milford, CT: Maggid Books, 2010), 78.

9. Austin Farrer, *The Crown of the Year: Weekly Paragraphs for the Holy Sacrament* (London: Dacre, 1952), 9.

10. N. T. Wright, *The Day the Revolution Began: Reconsidering the Meaning of Jesus's Crucifixion* (San Francisco: HarperOne, 2016).

11. Joan Didion, *The Year of Magical Thinking* (New York: Vintage Books, 2005), 56.

12. Alan E. Lewis, *Between Cross and Resurrection: A Theology of Holy Saturday* (Grand Rapids, MI: Eerdmans, 2001), 3.

13. C. S. Lewis, *A Grief Observed* (New York: Bantam Books, 1976), 1.

Easter

1. Søren Kierkegaard, *Journals*, ed. and trans. by Alexander Dru (New York: Harper Torchbooks, 1959), 252.

2. Robert J. Morgan, *Then Sings My Soul* (Nashville, TN: Thomas Nelson, 2003), 81.

Epilogue

1. T. S. Eliot, "East Coker," in "Four Quartets," *T.S. Eliot, Collected Poems, 1909–1962* (New York: Harcourt Brace Jovanovich, 1963), 182.